West Hills College
Funding for this book
provided by a grant
from **TANF**.
Cathy Barabe,
Director of Grants…
April 2000

HOW TO PREPARE FOR COLLEGE

Second Edition

Marjorie Eberts
Margaret Gisler

VGM Career Horizons
NTC/Contemporary Publishing Group

Library of Congress Cataloging-in-Publication Data

Eberts, Marjorie.
    How to prepare for college / Marjorie Eberts and Margaret
Gisler.—2nd ed.
        p.   cm.
    Includes bibliographical references (p.).
    ISBN 0-8442-0433-1
    1. Universities and colleges—Admission.   2. Study skills.
3. Education, Secondary.   I. Gisler, Margaret.   II. Title.
LB2351.E24   1999
378.1'61'0973—dc21   99-11645
                                          CIP

Published by VGM Career Horizons
A division of NTC/Contemporary Publishing Group, Inc.
4255 West Touhy Avenue, Lincolnwood (Chicago), Illinois 60646-1975 U.S.A.
Copyright © 1999, 1990 by NTC/Contemporary Publishing Group, Inc.
Printed in the United States of America
International Standard Book Number: 0-8442-0433-1

99 00 01 02 03 04 VL 18 17 16 15 14 13 12 11 10 9 8 7 6 5 4 3 2 1

To our children—Martha, Ken, Maria, Ann, Mark, and David—who prepared diligently and were admitted to the colleges that were right for each of them.

Contents

**Deal Effectively with College
Acceptance and Rejection
Notices 242**

**Appendix A: Suggested Reference
Books 247**

**Appendix B: Suggested Web
Sites 252**

Appendix C: Glossary 256

About the Authors

Marjorie Eberts and Margaret Gisler have been writing together professionally for nineteen years. They are prolific free-lance authors with more than sixty books in print. Their writing is usually in the field of education. The two authors have written textbooks, beginning readers, and study skills books for schoolchildren. Besides writing books, the two authors have a syndicated education column, "Dear Teacher," which appears in newspapers throughout the country, and have recently extended their advice giving to the Internet. Their column gives parents advice on how to guide their children successfully through school in order to prepare them for college.

Eberts is a graduate of Stanford University, and Gisler is a graduate of Ball State and Butler Universities. Both received their specialist degrees in education from Butler University. The two authors are also teachers with more than twenty years of teaching experience between them.

Writing this book was a special pleasure for the authors as it gave them the opportunity to help more students prepare for college.

HOW TO SUCCEED IN HIGH SCHOOL

Students who learn how to succeed in high school will succeed in college.

Get Everything You Can from High School

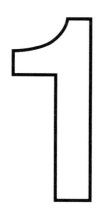

High school is your dress rehearsal for college. It's where you learn how to do many of the things that you will need to do to succeed in college. Look at the similarities between high school and college. In both high school and college you will need to

- study and do well on tests;

- do homework;

- take notes in class;

- participate in class discussions;

- write term papers;

- give speeches; and

- balance your academic, social, and work responsibilities.

Laying the Groundwork for College in High School

The more successfully you handle your high school years, the more prepared you will be for college. For example, if you write several term papers in high school, you will not be overwhelmed when faced with your first term paper assignment in college. Furthermore, if you learn how to take lecture notes in high school, you will feel comfortable in college classes where lecturing is often the major method of instruction. You will know how to listen for and write down what is important.

A successful college experience depends on more than your academic skills. Students who learn how to divide their time between schoolwork, extracurricular activities, jobs, and social demands in high school will know how to handle the many conflicting demands on their time at college. Students who set and achieve goals during their high school years will find it easy to set goals for themselves in college. In the same way, students who have been thinking while in high school about possible career choices will find career decisions much simpler to make in college. Finally, students who carefully plan their high school curriculum will find it easier to be admitted to college. In this chapter you will find out about the steps you need to take while you are in high school in order to prepare for college.

Determining Your Goals

You can drift through high school never setting goals, never feeling motivated to do a good job, and never thinking about how you could improve yourself. If you do this, you will not get all you can out of your high school years nor will you acquire the necessary habits to be successful in college.

Setting long-term goals

You need to know in high school where you are going in the future. You don't have to know exactly what you would like to do, but you should have some idea. Long-term goals will give you direction and motivate you to accomplish the tasks that are essential for succeeding in high school. For example, students who are thinking about becoming lawyers or actors will want to do well in speech class. On the other hand, students who see the speech class as just a graduation requirement may not be as motivated to do well in the class.

You can daydream about your long-term goals. It can even be motivating to imagine what it would be like to be in college or following a certain career path. Remember, however, that dreams are wishes, and wishes don't always come true.

Can you answer the following questions with "Yes"?

- Are you planning to attend college?

- Have you thought about what career you would like to pursue?

If you answered "Yes" to both questions, then you have begun to develop long-term goals that will influence much of what you do in high school. For example, if you are planning to attend college, you will choose your high school classes with that goal in mind. If you are thinking of a career as a newspaper reporter, you will probably want to work on the school newspaper.

Setting short-term goals

Having long-term career goals helps you set many of your short-term goals. These are the goals that can be accomplished within a week or a few months. It takes years to accomplish the long-term goal of becoming an astronaut—a goal that requires college and additional years of training. But becoming an astronaut also requires accomplishing such short-term goals as making the honor roll, passing next week's test in chemistry, and doing tomorrow's geometry problems correctly.

In order to be admitted to college, most students will need to accomplish the majority of the following short-term goals. Check those goals that you have accomplished:

_____ learned what several colleges are like

_____ researched what high school courses are required for college entrance

_____ prepared for college entrance tests

_____ participated in extracurricular activities

Goals need to be specific. Long-term goals can be a bit fuzzy, but short-term goals need to be quite specific. While it is admirable to have the goal of becoming a better student during the fall semester, such a goal is so broad that it is difficult to achieve. The goal of spending two hours on your studies each evening is more specific and should help you become a better student.

Goals need to be achievable. When you set goals, you also need to make sure that they are achievable. The goal of receiving an A on the biology final is quite realistic if you have been doing good work in the class. However, if you haven't studied biology very seriously during the school year and have been getting Ds in the subject on all your report cards, such a goal will be very difficult to achieve.

If you don't make short-term goals that are both specific and achievable, you will be discouraged by your efforts to meet them. Decide which of the following goals most students could expect to achieve.

_____ make straight As

_____ pass a biology quiz

_____ arrive at school on time every day

_____ learn how to diagram sentences

_____ win a National Merit Scholarship

Achieving your goals

You are constantly setting short-term goals in order to complete high school successfully and prepare for college and a future career. Both short-term and long-term goals can seem impossible to realize unless they are broken down into manageable steps. You can compare reaching a goal to climbing a ladder. Each step puts you closer to the top and motivates you to continue your climb.

When you write a term paper, you go through a number of steps like the following. You should break down any goal that you wish to reach in the same organized way.

Goal: Complete a term paper

- select topic

- research term paper

- outline term paper

- write rough draft

- revise rough draft

- write final draft

- proofread final draft

- turn in term paper

Goal: Prepare for a college entrance test.

One goal that almost every college-bound high school student has is to do well on the SAT I or ACT. List some of the steps that you will take to accomplish this goal.

_____

_____

_____

_____

_____

Remember: It is having a little belief in yourself, setting achievable goals, and working steadily to achieve each one that will help you reach most of your goals.

Determining What Colleges Will Expect from You

You want to go to college, but in order to go to college you have to be admitted to one. Knowing the four most important requirements that colleges expect in applicants will help you set goals that will give you the qualifications to be admitted to college.

As you read about what counts toward being admitted to college, think about colleges that you might attend. Then for each category write down one or more goals that will help you gain admission to a college that interests you. If you are a freshman or sophomore or even a junior, you have time to set and achieve goals that will help you be admitted to college. Even seniors can improve their chances for admission by having an outstanding year.

Your grades. This is probably the most important factor in your admission to college and placement in certain majors. Most colleges have minimum standards that you must meet. The more selective the college is, the higher your grades need to be.

Grade point average I need for college admission: _____

My grade point average: _____

Goals: _____

_____

_____

_____

_____

_____

_____

_____

_____

Your test scores. Most colleges will require you to take either the SAT I or ACT for admission. In addition, you will probably need to achieve certain minimum scores for admission. Preparation for these tests will help you score better on them.

Test scores I need for college admission:

ACT composite score: _____ SAT I verbal: _____

SAT I mathematics: _____

My test scores: _____

Goals: _____

_____

_____

_____

_____

_____

_____

_____

_____

Your activities. The quality of your participation in school and community activities rather than the quantity of your memberships and activities is what colleges are interested in. They would rather you were a debating or fencing champion than someone who has dabbled in many activities and not gained any particular expertise. Colleges also like to see that you have shown concern for others through volunteering.

My major extracurricular activities: _____

_____

_____

_____

_____

Goals: _____

_____

_____

_____

_____

_____

_____

_____

_____

Your work experience. Colleges are interested in your work experience as another dimension of your abilities. It can be a negative factor if working has hurt your grades.

My jobs: _____

_____

_____

_____

Goals: _____

_____

_____

_____

_____

_____

_____

_____

Exploring Possible Careers

In order to set long-term career goals, you must know yourself and something about a variety of possible careers. Knowing yourself, in this case, means being aware of what your interests and strengths are. Take a few minutes right now to write down some information about yourself.

My main interests in life right now:

_____

_____

The three high school classes I have found most interesting:

_____

_____

Four things that I do unusually well (this could include making friends, concentrating for long periods of time, or solving math problems):

1. _____

2. _____

3. _____

4. _____

Look over what you have just written, for it will give you clues about what type of career path to follow. Most people who have successful careers are doing things that interest them and work in areas in which they have skills. If you wrote down that you like tennis, swimming, and soccer, enjoyed your biology class, and are unusually skilled in most sports, you might want to consider a career in sports medicine or coaching, for example. Now list some career goals that tie in with what you have discovered about yourself.

Possible career goals: _____

_____

_____

_____

_____

_____

_____

_____

_____

_____

Investigating careers

There are thousands of different careers that you could follow, but there simply isn't time to thoroughly investigate more than a few of them. You should limit your investigation to those careers that tie in more closely to your interests and abilities. There are a number of steps you can take during high school to find out about a variety of careers. The more information you have, the better the decision you will be able to make.

Participate in school career days. By attending high school career days, you will get an overview of several careers. You will usually find out about such job characteristics as education requirements, training, wage scales, and opportunities for advancement.

Talk to your counselors. You don't have to do everything by yourself. Counselors can help you think of considerations that you may have overlooked. They can also be of considerable assistance in helping you plan the courses that will help you realize your career goals.

Talk to people working in different careers. People who are working in a career can share with you how they started in that career and what they like and dislike about it. You can't find this type of personal information in a book.

Join career clubs. At your high school and in the community, there are clubs that are devoted to the exploration of careers. These clubs help you meet people working in different careers and may even help you get part-time jobs to sample a career more closely. Some of these clubs are Junior Achievement Inc., National 4-H Council, Boys Clubs of America, Distributive Education Clubs of America, and Future Homemakers of America.

Get a part-time job. If a career as a hospital administrator interests you, try to get a part-time job at a hospital rather than at a fast food restaurant. Working in a particular job is the best way to find out whether you would like it as a career.

Thinking about the future

Once you have found one or more careers that you might like to follow, you should think about the steps you need to take in the years to come in order to follow these careers. Answer the following questions about each career that you are considering:

What should I be doing two years from now to prepare myself to follow this career?

_____

_____

_____

_____

_____

_____

_____

_____

What should I be doing four years from now to prepare myself to follow this career?

_____

_____

_____

_____

_____

_____

_____

_____

Picking your classes wisely

You know where you are going when you leave your home. You have a route and you follow it. If you have any doubts about where you are going, you probably look at a map or ask someone for directions.

When you have the goal of going to college, you have to know the route that will help you accomplish that goal. One part of that route is the classes that you take in high school. If you don't select the right classes, you may find that you are not able to get into the college of your choice. Furthermore, you may find that you have not even taken the classes necessary for high school graduation or essential for preparing yourself for a career that interests you.

Getting the advice you need

Just as it is smart to ask for directions when you are taking a trip into an unfamiliar area, it is smart to ask for advice when you are preparing for college or a career—unfamiliar areas to you. Obviously, your high school counselor should be one of your primary advisors. You will also find that your parents, older brothers and sisters, and friends who are in high school and college can give you very helpful advice.

The time to consult with these advisors is before you even enter high school. Then you may be sure to select a course of study that will meet high school graduation, college entrance, and career requirements. You should talk to these advisors once each year to make sure that the courses you select are the ones that meet your current needs.

Counselors. Your high school counselors are the experts on high school graduation requirements and will know the entrance requirements for most colleges in your state. The counselors will also help you select a class load that is neither too easy nor too difficult.

Parents. Your parents or guardians probably know how you handle demands on your time. They can help you select a class load that will give you sufficient time to study and time for jobs, tasks at home, and school and community activities.

Older brothers and sisters and friends. These people know what high school is like. They have taken some of the courses that you will be taking. Ask them what these courses were like and what they got out of them. If any of your friends or siblings are in college, find out what high school courses helped them in college and what courses could have helped them.

Selecting your high school courses

The courses that you take in high school fall into two groups: required and elective. In the required category are the classes that you must take for high school graduation and college entrance. In the elective category are the classes you take for career preparation and your own personal enjoyment.

High school graduation requirements. These requirements are set by the state and your own high school. Complete the Courses Required for High School Graduation chart adding any additional courses in the space provided. Then check off each requirement as you meet it.

College entrance requirements. Different colleges have different entrance requirements. The individual college

Courses Required for High School Graduation

Required courses	Ninth grade		Tenth grade		Eleventh grade		Twelfth grade	
	Required	Completed	Required	Completed	Required	Completed	Required	Completed
English								
Mathematics								
Science								
U.S. History								
Social Studies								
Physical Education								

catalogs will tell you exactly what is required. Most colleges will require you to take a program that includes the following courses:

- four years of English;

- three or four years of college preparatory mathematics;

- two years of science with lab experience;

- at least two years of one foreign language; and

- at least two years of courses in the social sciences.

In addition, colleges expect students to have some exposure to the fine and performing arts and an introduction to computers. At many high schools, courses in these areas are required for graduation.

Cautions. Keep these points in mind:

- Colleges look at the *types* of courses that you take to meet their requirements. You need to build a strong *academic* background. Serious courses such as world history are preferred to light ones such as the history of television.

- Colleges prefer students to take four years of rigorous academic classes. They frown upon admitting students who take easy class loads any one of their four years in high school, especially the senior year.

- Some college majors have specific course requirements, so consider this information when you are determining what courses to take in high school.

If you know exactly which college you wish to attend, use its entrance requirements to complete the Courses Required for College Entrance chart. Otherwise, use the entrance requirements for any state university or more selective school, depending upon which type of school you think you will be attending. Check off each requirement as you complete it.

You want to start this chart in ninth grade to make sure that you complete all of the necessary courses for admission to college. You don't want to discover when you are a senior that you have not taken the appropriate courses for admission to the college of your choice.

Courses Required for College Entrance

Name of course	Number of years of study required	High school courses completed			
		9	10	11	12
English					
Mathematics					
Science					
Social Studies					
Foreign language					

Career preparation courses. Once you have made a tentative decision about the career or careers to pursue in the future, you should take some classes in those areas. This will help you decide whether you are truly interested. It will also help you prepare for such a career or careers. For example, someone who wants to become an engineer needs

Career Preparation Courses

Possible career   Courses helpful in preparing for this career

_____ _____ _____ _____

_____ _____ _____ _____

_____ _____ _____ _____

_____ _____ _____ _____

to take classes in mathematics and science, while a future health care professional needs to enroll in biology.

On the Career Preparation Courses chart on page 16 write down the courses that you think might help you prepare for the careers that you are considering.

Your four-year plan

By making a four-year plan of the courses that you will take in high school, you are setting out the route that will lead to your admission to college. Without such a plan, you may overlook a course that is necessary for college admission.

Use the information that you have written down in the sections on graduation requirements, college admission requirements' and career preparation courses to complete your four-year plan. No matter what school year you are in right now, you should complete all four years of the plan. Then carefully evaluate your plan and make any necessary changes before you complete your registration for classes each year.

Four-Year Plan of Courses

Ninth grade

First semester	Second semester
Required courses	Required courses
Elective courses	Elective courses

Tenth grade

First semester	Second semester
Required courses	Required courses
Elective courses	Elective courses

Eleventh grade

First semester	Second semester
Required courses	Required courses
Elective courses	Elective courses

Twelfth grade

First semester	Second semester
Required courses	Required courses
Elective courses	Elective courses

Improve Your Study Skills Now

Since your very first day of school, you have spent a great deal of time studying, from learning how to color within the lines to finding the area of a circle. And with each passing year, you have had more and more material to study. But have you learned *how* to study? Studying isn't a natural process like walking, breathing, or eating. It has to be learned. Unfortunately, few schools actually teach students how to study. Without this skill, students find learning far more difficult in high school and college than it should be.

Studying takes much time and energy. It is not a pleasant activity for most students. You can probably think of hundreds of other things that you would rather do. How often do you do these things instead of study? To become really interested in studying, you need to tie it closely to accomplishing your goals of going to college and preparing for a career. You need to have a reason for studying.

In this chapter you will learn how to organize your study place and time. You will also learn what basic study skills you need to have for high school and college as well as the special skills you need for different courses. Learning how to study now while you are in high school will make your high school and college years more enjoyable and successful as well as eliminate the stress that accompanies not knowing how to handle your schoolwork.

Rating Your Study Skills

Spending hours studying every day does not necessarily mean that you have good study skills. Nor does getting good grades mean that you have good study skills. Find out how your study skills rate by completing the Study Skills Evaluation.

Study Skills Evaluation

Put a check mark in the blank that best describes the way you study.

	Always	Sometimes	Never	
Study place				
I	_____	_____	_____	study in the same place at home.
I	_____	_____	_____	study in the same place at school.
I	_____	_____	_____	organize my study area.
I	_____	_____	_____	have supplies in my study area.
Study time				
I	_____	_____	_____	follow a study schedule.
I	_____	_____	_____	study every day.
I	_____	_____	_____	study for more than one hour every day.
I	_____	_____	_____	do my hardest assignments first.
I	_____	_____	_____	review after every class.
I	_____	_____	_____	review on days when I have no homework.

	Always	Sometimes	Never	
I	_____	_____	_____	schedule a weekly review session.

Basic study skills

	Always	Sometimes	Never	
I	_____	_____	_____	use different study methods for different subjects.
I	_____	_____	_____	concentrate when I study.
I	_____	_____	_____	have a list of my daily assignments.
I	_____	_____	_____	write my future assignments on a calendar.
I	_____	_____	_____	use the SQ3R (survey, question, read, recite, review) technique when I study.
I	_____	_____	_____	use a dictionary when I study.
I	_____	_____	_____	take notes when I study.
I	_____	_____	_____	get help when I have trouble understanding something.
I	_____	_____	_____	use the correct form when writing an outline.

Classroom study skills

	Always	Sometimes	Never	
I	_____	_____	_____	take notes during class time.
I	_____	_____	_____	review my class notes.
I	_____	_____	_____	listen attentively during class discussions.
I	_____	_____	_____	participate actively in class discussions.
I	_____	_____	_____	use textbook aids.
I	_____	_____	_____	turn in my assignments on time.

Interpreting your evaluation

Look back over the check marks you made in rating your study skills in four different areas. Ideally, most of your answers were "Always" or "Sometimes," indicating that you have good study skills. Every "Never" answer shows where there is a weakness in your study skills. The area with the most "Always" answers is the one where you have the best study skills, while the one with the most "Never" answers is your weakest. Keep your "Never" answers in mind as you read through this chapter and the next one so that you can find out how to acquire the study skills that you need. The better your study skills are, the more efficiently you learn.

Improving your study skills

Your study skills cannot be improved overnight; nor can they be improved by setting fuzzy goals. You need to set specific short-term goals in order to acquire the skills that you need. Acquiring skills like keeping a list of assignments, reviewing after every class, and participating actively in class discussions can dramatically improve the way you study. Begin to improve your study skills by selecting three skills beside which you placed check marks in the "Never" column and make it your goal to acquire those skills within four weeks. Keep track of your progress on the Study Skills Goals chart:

Study Skills Goals

Today's date: _____

Study goal 1: _____

_____

_____

_____

_____

Date in four weeks: _____

Improvement noted: _____

_____

_____

_____

Today's date: _____

Study goal 2: _____

_____

_____

_____

_____

Date in four weeks: _____

Improvement noted: _____

_____

_____

_____

_____

Today's date: _____

Study goal 3: _____

_____

_____

_____

_____

Date in four weeks: _____

Improvement noted: _____

_____

_____

_____

_____

Identifying Your Learning Style

An important part of knowing how to study lies in knowing how you best learn. Did you know that everyone does not learn in the same way? Everyone has his or her own distinct learning style. Your learning style is different from your best friend's and even your brother's or sister's. You need to find out what your own personal learning style is so that you can use it when you are studying.

Completing your learning style questionnaire

Complete the Learning Style Questionnaire to find out more about your personal learning style.

Learning Style Questionnaire

Circle the answers that best complete the following statements.

1. I remember things best when I study
    a. early in the morning.
    b. at school.
    c. in the afternoon after school.
    d. after dinner.
    e. late at night.

2. I study best when I am
    a. with one friend.
    b. alone.
    c. with a study group.
    d. with the teacher.
    e. sometimes alone and sometimes with a friend.
    f. with an adult.

3. The things I learn best I learn by
    a. reading them.
    b. writing them down.
    c. hearing them.
    d. reading and writing them.
    e. reading and hearing them.
    f. writing and hearing them.
    g. reading, writing, *and* hearing them.

4. The things I learn best I learn through
    a. my eyes.
    b. my ears.
    c. my touch.
    d. a combination of _____.

5. I study best when the lighting is

    a. strong.

    b. of average intensity.

    c. very low.

    d. sunlight.

6. I concentrate best when my study area is

    a. hot.

    b. warm.

    c. cool.

    d. so cold that I need to wear a sweater.

7. I study best

    a. sitting in a comfortable chair.

    b. sitting at a desk.

    c. sitting or lying on the floor.

    d. sitting or lying on a bed.

8. I concentrate best when

    a. there is no noise.

    b. it is relatively quiet.

    c. there is light background noise.

    d. there is considerable noise.

    e. the television is on.

9. To study best, I need

    a. to eat as I study.

    b. to have just eaten.

    c. to be hungry.

    d. to chew gum.

    e. to drink water or soda.

    f. to have no food or beverage.

10. To study best, I

    a. study for a long period of time.

    b. study for at least one hour.

    c. study at least thirty minutes at a time.

    d. study at least fifteen minutes at a time.

Creating your personal learning profile

Look back over the answers that you circled. Now use these answers to create your own learning profile. This profile will give you a picture of how you learn best.

Learning Profile

Environmental needs (5, 6, 7, 8)

I study best when

the lighting is _____,

the temperature is _____,

the sound level is _____,

and the place I am working at is _____.

Social needs (2)

I study best when I am _____.

Sensory needs (3, 4)

I study best when the senses(s) I mainly use is (are) my

_____, and I learn by _____.

Physical needs (1, 9, 10)

I study best when my study time is _____,

the amount of time I study is _____,

and the food or drink I am consuming is _____

_____.

Creating the Best Study Area

You don't need a fancy study area, but you do need to establish one place for doing most of your studying. This place does not have to be a soundproof cell. However, it shouldn't be a recreational area either. It does not matter if the study place you select for yourself is at home, at school, or in a library as long as you usually study in that same place. The importance of studying in the same place is that you don't waste time and energy adjusting to new sights, sounds, smells, and distractions every time you study.

If you don't already have a study area, select one now. Try to select an area that is away from traffic and distractions. It should be a place where you believe you will be able to get your studying done.

I plan to do most of my studying in _____

_____.

Choosing the best conditions

Now that you have selected your study area, you need to make sure that the area meets all the environmental conditions under which you learn best. You may find it helpful to go back and look at your learning profile.

Sound level. Noise can distract you from studying. Even background noise can cause problems if you are not used to the noise. Try to lower the volume if you like to study with music playing, for research shows if it's too loud it will disrupt your studying. However, if you find that soft music helps drown out other interfering noises in your study area or that it helps to keep your mind focused, make sure you have it.

Lights. When you are setting up lighting in your study area, take into account the direction from which any daylight or artificial light will fall. Avoid glare. The best way to avoid glare is to have the main light source come from the side. Try to have good lighting over your books at all times. Very bright or very dim light, even if you prefer it, can cause eye strain.

Temperature. The temperature of your study area affects your learning. If it is too hot, you may find it easy to fall asleep. On the other hand, if it is too cold, you will find it hard to concentrate on anything except getting warm. The ideal temperature for a study area is usually approximately 70°F (21°C).

Comfort. Your comfort as you study is important. Make sure that your study area has whatever you need to study best—a comfortable chair, a desk and chair, or a bed.

Air circulation. Is the air circulation good in the place you have chosen as your study area? You need a good supply of oxygen to be mentally and physically alert as you study.

Having a good work surface

Your study area needs to be a place where you can do written assignments. Even if you do most of your studying while lying on the floor, you still need to have a good work surface in your study area. It should be in a spot where distractions won't interrupt your studying—against a wall may be better than in front of a window, for example.

The work surface should be at a height that will let you do your work in a comfortable position. Your chair should provide good support for your lower back and shoulders. A chair without this support will cause you to tire quickly.

The top of the work surface should be large enough to hold everything that you need while studying. Most students know that they need their books and notebooks but forget they may need a calculator, typewriter, or computer. List the materials that you will need on your work surface:

_____   _____   _____

_____   _____   _____

You should also have a storage area near your work surface so that you can reach all your supplies without having to get up and down like a yo-yo.

Equipping your study area

Make sure that your study area has all the supplies that you need before you begin using it. Otherwise, you will be constantly interrupting your study sessions to find the supplies you need. Check over the following supply list. Add any additional items that you feel you need to complete your list.

Basic supplies	Have	Need to have
atlas	_____	_____
calculator	_____	_____
colored paper	_____	_____
colored pencils	_____	_____
compass	_____	_____
computer	_____	_____
computer disks	_____	_____
computer paper	_____	_____
correction fluid	_____	_____
crayons	_____	_____
dictionary	_____	_____
encyclopedias	_____	_____
erasers	_____	_____
felt tip pens	_____	_____
folders	_____	_____
glue	_____	_____
graph paper	_____	_____
highlighter pens	_____	_____
index cards	_____	_____
marking pens	_____	_____
paper	_____	_____
pencil sharpener	_____	_____
pencils	_____	_____
rubber bands	_____	_____
ruler	_____	_____

scissors   _____   _____

scotch tape   _____   _____

scrap paper   _____   _____

stapler   _____   _____

stencils   _____   _____

thesaurus   _____   _____

typewriter   _____   _____

typing paper   _____   _____

_____   _____   _____

_____   _____   _____

_____   _____   _____

_____   _____   _____

Checking your study area

Review your learning profile once more to make sure that
your study area meets your environmental needs for
learning. Look around your study area and remove any
objects that you could find distracting. You should also
take away other items that are not necessary and that
cause clutter. Check to see if you have purchased all the
supplies that you need and that they have been stored
close to your work surface.

Using your study area

As you start to use your study area, you will find things
that need to be changed. You will also find there are
distractions that annoy you, such as a noisy water sprin-
kler or a constantly ringing telephone. Make a list of these
distractions and then try to think of the best way to eliminate each one as quickly as possible.

No study area, even your own, can be perfect. If you
follow the guidelines in this section for setting up your
study area, you should have a place where you can work
faster, feel more alert, and have more productive study time.

Remember, your physical health also plays an important part in your studying. So you should try to get enough sleep and eat three well-balanced meals a day. Being hungry or tired can affect the quality of your study time even if all the environmental conditions are close to perfect for you.

Squeezing Study Time into Your Busy Schedule

You have set up your own study place, and now you need to find the time to use it. Did you know that there are 168 hours in a week? For quite a few of those hours you are busy eating, sleeping, and going to school. What are you doing with the rest of your time? You control much of what you do with this time. How much of it are you using for studying and activities that really matter to you?

Your time is one of your most important resources. You should know how you are using it and plan to use it productively. Fill out the Weekly Time Chart of Activities so you can see at a glance where all your hours are going. Describe your activities every half hour from the time you get up until you go to bed. Be specific. Tell exactly what you are doing—talking on the telephone, watching television, reading.

Weekly Time Chart of Activities

Hours	Activity						
	Monday	Tuesday	Wednesday	Thursday	Friday	Saturday	Sunday
Morning **6:30–7:00**							
7:00–7:30							
7:30–8:00							
8:00–8:30							
8:30–9:00							
9:00–9:30							
9:30–10:00							
10:00–10:30							
10:30–11:00							
11:00–11:30							
11:30–12:00							
12:00–12:30							

Hours	Activity						
	Monday	Tuesday	Wednesday	Thursday	Friday	Saturday	Sunday
Afternoon 12:30–1:00							
1:00–1:30							
1:30–2:00							
2:00–2:30							
2:30–3:00							
3:00–3:30							
3:30–4:00							
4:00–4:30							
4:30–5:00							
5:00–5:30							
5:30–6:00							
6:00–6:30							

Hours	Activity						
	Monday	Tuesday	Wednesday	Thursday	Friday	Saturday	Sunday
Evening 6:30–7:00							
7:00–7:30							
7:30–8:00							
8:00–8:30							
8:30–9:00							
9:00–9:30							
9:30–10:00							
10:00–10:30							
10:30–11:00							
11:00–11:30							
11:30–12:00							

Analyzing how you spend your time

Look back over your time chart to see how much time you devoted to the activities listed in the Time Use Analysis chart. This will give you a better idea of how you spend your time.

Time Use Analysis

Required activities	Hours spent on activity
Time spent at school:	_____
Time spent sleeping:	_____
Time spent in after-school activities:	_____
Time spent eating:	_____
Time spent working:	_____
Time spent studying:	_____
Total time spent on required activities:	_____

Other activities	
Time spent visiting with friends:	_____
Time spent visiting with family:	_____
Time spent watching television:	_____
Time spent talking on the telephone:	_____
Time spent on no particular activity:	_____
Total time spent on other activities:	_____

Your time. Were you surprised by how you actually spent your time? Do you think your time was well used? Your study time is important but so is concentrating on extracurricular activities. Was too much of your time frittered away not doing anything special?

Study time. Are you spending enough time studying? In college you will be expected to spend at least one hour studying for every hour in class. In high school you should spend enough time studying to complete all your assignments, to review your schoolwork daily, and to study for quizzes and tests. For most students, this means at least an hour of studying outside of school each day. However, two hours is a more appropriate amount of time for serious students.

Planning more productive use of your time

With a little planning, you can create a schedule that will help you use your time more productively. If you don't have definite times for studying, then you probably will put it off. For example, maybe you put off doing math by watching television before dinner, talking on the phone after dinner, fixing a snack, and so on. Then you try to do the problems right before you go to bed or tell yourself that you will get up in the morning and do them.

Having a definite time to study each day—not necessarily the same time—gives you the organized approach to studying that you will need for college. In college no one will tell you when to study—it is completely up to you. Learning to arrange your study time in high school will makes it much easier to handle the greater freedom in college. Just as you need to schedule your study time, you need to schedule time for activities that are important to you. You need time for tennis lessons, practicing the piano, and volunteer activities, for example.

Good time management will

- save you time;

- give you more time to relax;

- give you time to concentrate on your interests;

- give you time to do more things;

- improve your study habits, and

- give a sense of purpose to your days.

Can you really afford to pass up the benefits of scheduling your time?

Beginning your time schedule. Look for the pitfalls in how you have been spending your time, according to the Weekly Time Chart of Activities, before starting to create a time schedule. Ask yourself the following questions:

1. Did I plan my study time in advance?   Yes   No

2. Did I study before class?   Yes   No

3. Did I study right after class?   Yes   No

4. Did social activities interrupt my studying? Yes   No

5. Did I build in regular time for reviewing? Yes   No

6. Did I make time for extra projects?   Yes   No

7. Did I have to cram?   Yes   No

8. Did I have time to relax?   Yes   No

9. Did I have free time?   Yes   No

10. Did I get enough sleep?   Yes   No

Every "No" answer is a pitfall you will want to avoid when creating your time schedule.

Basic guidelines. Regardless of your year in high school there are some basic guidelines you need to follow in planning your time schedule:

- Use your schedule to meet your goals.

- Consider your study priorities. (Which classes need more time?)

- Plan study times before or right after classes when possible.

- Plan for emergencies.

- Schedule adequate time for study—neither too little nor too much.

- Build in time for review.

- Block off time for projects.

- Schedule sufficient free time.

- Build in flexibility.

Some time considerations. Keep in mind that you will remember more after five one-hour study sessions spread over a week than after one five-hour cram session. You should try to study every major subject at least half an hour per day. On weekends, you can schedule time for classes that are giving you problems.

There is no one time of day when everyone should study. How you should schedule your study time depends on your learning style. Most people have times when they function at their best—those are the best study times.

Your study schedule. Complete the Personal Study Schedule. Keep all the guidelines and time considerations in mind as you make your schedule. Write down all your scheduled activities; then allot time for studying and special activities. The remaining time should be free time. You don't want to schedule every minute of your life.

Personal Study Schedule

Hours	Activity						
	Monday	Tuesday	Wednesday	Thursday	Friday	Saturday	Sunday
Morning **6:00–6:30**							
6:30–7:00							
7:00–7:30							
7:30–8:00							
8:00–8:30							
8:30–9:00							
9:00–9:30							
9:30–10:00							
10:00–10:30							
10:30–11:00							
11:00–11:30							
11:30–12:00							

Hours	Activity						
	Monday	Tuesday	Wednesday	Thursday	Friday	Saturday	Sunday
Afternoon **12:00–12:30**							
12:30–1:00							
1:00–1:30							
1:30–2:00							
2:00–2:30							
2:30–3:00							
3:00–3:30							
3:30–4:00							
4:00–4:30							
4:30–5:00							
5:00–5:30							
5:30–6:00							

Hours	Activity						
	Monday	Tuesday	Wednesday	Thursday	Friday	Saturday	Sunday
Evening 6:00–6:30							
6:30–7:00							
7:00–7:30							
7:30–8:00							
8:00–8:30							
8:30–9:00							
9:00–9:30							
9:30–10:00							
10:00–10:30							
10:30–11:00							
11:00–11:30							
11:30–12:00							

Following your schedule. A study schedule has no value unless you follow it. If your schedule seems impossible to follow, you may be scheduling too much of your time. Keep adjusting your schedule until it works for you. You will approach your schoolwork with far more confidence when you have scheduled your time in a productive and manageable way.

Making Studying Easier

Good students are rarely puzzled about when an assignment is due, what the day's homework is, or where their study guide for a test is. They handle these day-to-day concerns by using aids that make their studying far easier and more efficient. They also know how to use such aids as computers, calculators, encyclopedias, dictionaries, and flash cards.

Calendar. Every student needs a calendar on which to record future assignments, appointments, and social events. You may have a project due in three weeks and believe you have ample time in which to get it done. However, you may also have several other assignments due during that time period and some important social engagements or a dental appointment. Time passes swiftly, and you may forget all your obligations and have to burn the midnight oil in order to get the project turned in on time. By using a calendar, you can plan for future events. You will know when to start preparing for tests and when to finish different parts of a project. You should have a calendar in your study area and should thumb through it at the start of every study session. A calendar banishes unpleasant surprises. If you are a computer buff, you can elect to keep your calendar on a computer.

Assignment notebook. You need to have a daily record of your assignments for every class. Take an assignment notebook to each class and write down the details of every assignment as well as the dates for quizzes and tests and the deadlines for turning in papers and projects. Check your assignment notebook before you leave school each day so that you take home all the books and materials that you will need. Then make sure that you always write all the dates and deadlines from your assignment notebook on your calendar and also on your weekly time schedule.

Daily "do" list. A list of what must be done each day will help you make sure that nothing is forgotten like an appointment with a counselor or a meeting after school. Check your calendar when you make up your list for each day.

Notebooks and folders. Every day you complete papers, complete study guides, and have quizzes and tests returned to you. Develop a system for keeping the papers for each class together—use separate folders or notebooks with sections for each class. Store the papers you are not currently using but will need later in folders in your study area.

Computer. The computer is a new aid for students. It makes writing papers a breeze because it is easier to make revisions and check your spelling and grammar. You will probably have to use a computer to write all of your papers when you are in college.

You can also use commercial programs to improve a variety of your skills such as spelling and mathematics. You can even prepare for the SAT I on the computer. Computer-assisted instruction (CAI) can actually teach you in a step-by-step approach such subjects as biology and history. The program keeps working with you until you have mastered the subject matter. At the end of each lesson it evaluates your performance. Your teacher should be able to suggest worthwhile programs.

Calculator. High school students use calculators in their advanced math and science classes. You will also need to use a calculator on college admissions tests and in college classes such as economics, statistics, and psychology. Use a calculator to eliminate your fears about accuracy in all of your calculations.

Encyclopedias. When you want to know the who, what, when, where, how, or why of almost anything in a very short time, the encyclopedia is the study aid that will give you a quick overview, whether it is in book or CD-ROM format.

Dictionary. Use the dictionary every time you have the slightest doubt about how a word is spelled or what it means.

Flash cards. When you have to memorize anything—from definitions to chemical formulas to words in a foreign language—flash cards are what you should use. They are also extremely helpful to use in preparing for all kinds of tests.

Boosting Your Study Skills

To do well in high school and prepare yourself for college, you need to know how you learn and to be a well organized student. But, you also have to know how to study, which includes knowing how to get the most out of your textbooks and being able to outline, take notes, and underline. You must master these basic study techniques and understand the importance of regular review of all your work.

How to use a textbook

Textbooks contain the information that most high school and college teachers expect their students to learn. Fortunately, textbooks are usually organized in a way that helps you learn information easily. What is important in a textbook is usually clearly emphasized.

Learn all the words in word lists at the start or end of a chapter as well as all the words in boldface or italic type. Once you know what these words mean, you have a clear understanding of the key concepts of a chapter. The headings give you a preview of each section so you always know what you are supposed to learn, while the summaries at the end of a chapter tell you what you should have learned. If you thoroughly understand the summary of a chapter, then you probably have mastered what you need to know in a chapter. It is easy to check your mastery: All you have to do is complete the exercises at the end of a chapter. As you study a chapter you should look at all the pictures, illustrations, and charts, for they will make the meaning of what is said much clearer.

Knowing what is in the different parts of a textbook helps you use it. The table of contents in the front of the book gives general information about what is covered in each chapter. The glossary is really a small dictionary of all the important terms used in the book. It gives the pronunciations and definitions of many of the technical words that you do not know. The index gives an alphabetical list of the topics covered in the textbook. And if you are looking for additional reading, you will usually find a bibliography in most textbooks that will provide you with a reading list.

Textbook aids. When you are having difficulty understanding a textbook, read the introduction carefully to find out if the publisher offers aids like study guides, workbooks, and extra problem sets. You will find these aids very helpful.

SQ3R—one way to study a textbook

One of the best ways to learn the material in a textbook is to use the SQ3R study technique. Your third or fourth grade teacher might have taught this technique to you, and, if so, you might have been using it ever since with every textbook that you have studied. The letters in SQ3R stand for the steps that you follow in studying a textbook.

S stands for survey. Begin by surveying a reading assignment. This means looking at all the headings and subheadings in the assigned material. This is the material that stands out in different type, either boldface or italic. Once you have a general picture of what you are to study, go on to the next step.

Q stands for question. Make a question for the first heading that asks what you are going to learn in that section. The question gives you a challenge—a reason to continue studying. You can also make questions for subheadings. Keep your questions for future study sessions. Make sure you leave room for your answer between each question written on a piece of paper.

R stands for read. After you have written your first question, read the material under the heading thoroughly and carefully to find the answer. Don't overlook the captions under photographs and illustrations. Take the time to look up any word that you do not know as you are reading.

R stands for recite. As soon as you have read and found the answer to your question, recite the answer out loud without looking at the text. For additional reinforcement, write down the answer to your question. Then follow the same steps for the remaining headings in your assignment.

R stands for review. Before putting your textbook away, review all the material you have covered during your study session. To review, skim over the headings again, recite the important ideas under each heading, and answer the questions you wrote. If there are any questions that you can't answer, reread the material as well as your answers. Then do any exercises that are included in the assigned material.

SQ3R's benefits. At first you may find the SQ3R technique very time consuming. However, if you repeat the review step a few hours after completing it the first time and every few days after that, you will find that you have really learned the material. Studying for a test will not need to consist of anything more than the last step of SQ3R. The more you use SQ3R, the quicker you will be able to use it and the more convinced you will become of the benefits of this study technique. Try it now over just this section on SQ3R. Reread the headings to survey the section. Then answer this question: How do you use SQ3R to study a textbook?

Outlining—another way to study a textbook

Textbooks are written from outlines. The main ideas of the outline are the major headings of the textbook, and the subheadings represent the supporting details. Outlining helps you group ideas together in such a way that you can clearly see the relationships between the main ideas and the details that support them. When you outline a textbook, you discover what the author or authors thought was important. At the same time, you create a tool that you can use in preparing for tests.

Follow a standard form when writing an outline. The major rule is that each division of an outline must have at least two subdivisions. Study the following outline to see if you really know how to organize one.

Title

I. Main idea

  A. Subtopic

    1. Major detail

      (a) Minor detail

        (1) Item supporting minor detail

        (2) Item supporting minor detail

      (b) Minor detail

    2. Major detail

  B. Subtopic

II. Main idea

  A. Subtopic

  B. Subtopic

Testing your outlining skills. See if you can complete the following outline for the first few pages of this chapter.

Learning How to Study in High School

I. Rating your study skills

  A. Interpreting your evaluation

  B. _____

    _____

II. _____

  _____

  A. Completing your learning style questionnaire

  B. _____

    _____

III. Creating the best study area

    A. _____

       _____

       1. sound level

       2. lights

       3. _____

       4. _____

       5. _____

    B. Having a good work surface

Avoid excessive detail. You can make outlines as detailed as you want, but be careful not to make your outline so detailed that you are almost rewriting the textbook.

Underlining and studying

College students often underline their textbooks and notebooks. It is difficult for high school students to get much experience in underlining since they usually don't buy the books they use in school and so cannot underline in them. Underlining, however, can help you when you review class notes, SQ3R notes, outlines, and study guides. Underline the key words, dates, definitions, and names that you need to remember. Just be discreet. If you get carried away with your underling, you will defeat the purpose of this technique. Underlining is especially useful after you have reviewed your SQ3R notes a few times. By then you will know most of the material so you can just underline the key points you need to remember—making reviewing a much simpler task. Practice underlining now by rereading and underlining this section on underlining and studying.

Taking notes

Taking notes while you are studying a textbook will reinforce what you are learning. In fact, the more senses that you use when studying, the easier it is for you to learn. Note taking involves writing down what you want to remember from what you are reading. Just don't make the mistake of writing out the whole textbook. Be very selective about what you write down.

College students often take notes right in the margins of their textbooks. You may find it helpful to take notes on binder paper so that you can rearrange your notes or insert any additional notes or information in your binder or notebook. Besides making frequent use of abbreviations in their notes, some students develop their own form of shorthand so they don't have to write as much. Try your hand at shortening the following common words. Just don't make your shorthand system so complicated that when you look back over your notes you cannot interpret them.

vocabulary: _____   encyclopedia: _____

high school: _____   textbook: _____

homework: _____   assignment: _____

Reviewing—a most important study technique

You know the importance of studying. You also must realize the importance of regularly reviewing your work in every class. Reviewing helps you remember what you studied today, yesterday, and last month. It is very easy to forget material that you have just studied. You need to review frequently your notes, outlines, study guides, and any other materials you have for each class. Your first review session should take place shortly after you have learned new material. Then you should review it a few days later. At least once a week you should spend time reviewing so that you can keep the total picture in your mind of what you are learning in each class. Your review periods do not need to be long—in fact, fifteen minutes should be sufficient for each subject.

Studying Different Subjects

Considering the number of years that you have been in school already, no one needs to tell you that every subject in school deals with different kinds of information. However, even students as experienced as you are often don't realize that each subject needs to be studied differently. You will find school quite difficult if you are studying English the same way you study science. It is somewhat like working on your golf swing in your physical education class and expecting it to improve your bowling score.

Not only does every subject have to be studied in a different way, but every subject has its own vocabulary. Match the following words to the subjects where you are most likely to find them.

Subject words	Subject
_____ numerator	a. social studies
_____ impeachment	b. English
_____ magma	c. science
_____ modifier	d. mathematics
_____ treaty	
_____ diameter	
_____ hyphen	

Studying mathematics

Mathematics is a subject in which you are constantly building on what you have learned earlier. You simply can't do complicated multiplication problems if your addition is shaky. Since each day's work is important, you must get in the habit of always doing your daily work. Furthermore, at the first sign of trouble you should seek help so you won't have a weak link in your math skills. You need to get a solid math background in high school because you will be using math in such college courses as psychology and economics and in almost every science class.

Math classes usually work in this way. A new topic is introduced in the textbook, your teacher does some sample problems, and then you are assigned some problems.

Preparation. To prepare yourself to do your assignment you should follow these steps:

- Take notes on your teacher's explanations.

- Copy each problem that your teacher puts on the board in your math notebook.

- Read the textbook and redo the sample problems.

- Review all your notes before beginning an assignment.

- Try to do your math assignments as soon after your math class as possible so that what you learned in class will be fresh in your mind.

Handling assignments. Use the following techniques while doing your assignments:

- Write numbers as neatly as you can.

- Get in the habit of using estimation to determine if your answers seem correct.

- If you run into difficulty with a problem, try substituting smaller numbers and then see if you can solve the problem.

- Read all story problems more than once. The last sentence will usually tell you what you are trying to find out. Draw diagrams when appropriate.

- Check your answers against answers in the textbook when possible.

Additional hints:

- Keep all old quizzes and tests to use when preparing for chapter and final tests. The test problems are likely to be similar. Prepare by redoing the problems.

- Learn to be proficient with the calculator.

Studying social studies

It simply isn't possible to call reading a section or chapter in a social studies textbook studying. Studying means being actively involved with what you are trying to learn. Use the SQ3R technique, outline the material, or take notes whenever you have an assignment in your social studies textbook.

To remember which events occurred before or after other events, get in the habit of creating timelines. And to memorize names, terms, and dates, use flash cards.

Studying science

Approach your study of science in a very organized way. Keep all textbook notes, class notes, and study guides for a chapter together as you will need to look at them when preparing for labs and studying for tests.

In science classes, you have to learn a great number of new words as well as formulas. Flash cards can be very helpful for this. As in social studies, you need to use SQ3R, outline, or take notes in order to learn the textbook material. It also helps to preview a section in a textbook before it is discussed in class so that you feel more at home with the new material.

Because a lot of difficult material is covered in science, study every science course daily and review frequently. You cannot afford to get behind in science classes because so much material is covered each day. On lab days, know what you are going to do before the session begins in order to understand fully the experiments you are going to do.

Studying a foreign language

Studying a foreign language involves learning three different skills at the same time: speaking, reading, and writing. So whenever you are working on one skill, try to reinforce it by using another at the same time. For example, when you are writing out an exercise, read it aloud.

It takes years to learn a foreign language. The language that you start learning in high school you may continue studying in college. Therefore, you may want to use your high school flash cards and notebooks in college. Start your vocabulary flash cards the first day you enter high school. At the same time start a notebook with sections on grammar and culture. If you use a binder, you can keep adding and rearranging pages.

Foreign languages are much like mathematics since both subjects are cumulative and everything you learn must be remembered. What you learn the first day in high school French you will be using in your junior year in college when you study in France.

Studying English

Most students take English classes during their first year in college. They also have to take a great number of essay tests during their college years. In order to be ready for college, you should know and be able to apply the rules of English grammar as well as be able to write essays, term papers, and reports.

During your high school years, concentrate on learning what you don't know about English. Every time you make a mistake in an exercise or receive red correction marks on a theme paper, find out exactly what you did wrong and learn how to correct your error.

Studying Successfully

By now you should have selected and set up your own study area. You should also be working on your time schedule. The five study tips that follow will make a difference in your learning:

Study what you don't know. Never waste time rereading or studying what you already know. Instead, make lists of what you don't know and study this material.

Review after every class. Your memory is short. You need to review as soon as possible after every class. This will help reinforce the material that you have just learned.

Schedule weekly review sessions. Review what is being covered in each grading period at least once a week. Reviewing strengthens your learning.

Get help fast. Whenever you don't understand something, get help immediately. You can talk to the teacher, a classmate, a parent, or a tutor.

Study every day. You need to study at least one hour every day now that you are in high school.

Learn the Tricks to Succeeding in the Classroom

You spend approximately 180 days every year in the classroom. Are you getting all you can from your time there? Is every day full of learning new things and acquiring important skills? Or are you frittering away your time with meaningless activities because you don't know how to ace the classroom experience?

Although you get your education in many places, the major place for acquiring an education right now is the classroom. Just attending class is not sufficient, although good attendance is certainly important. You must be an active participant in what is happening in the classroom. In this chapter, you will learn what you should be doing in the classroom to get the education that will prepare you for college and a career.

Achieve a Good Attendance Record

It is trite but true. The only person you are hurting is yourself when you cut class. In order to acquire a good high school education and be really prepared for college, you must attend all your classes regularly. When you miss class, you miss a major part of your education. You can catch up on missed material in the textbook, but you can never catch up on what was discussed in the classroom. You miss learning your teachers' and other students' feelings on issues. You miss explanations of concepts that go beyond what is written in textbooks. You miss the opportunity to experience change in your feelings and attitudes. And you also deprive the other students in your classes of your input. Attending class right before a test or near the end of the semester is especially important since teachers tend to stress what is essential to know at those times.

If you are sick or unable to attend class for a few days, make sure you get all the assignments. Ask the teacher if you can copy his or her notes or get notes from a student in the class who is good at recording what happens. It also helps to talk to a classmate about what was discussed in class in order to make the notes that you have read and copied come to life.

Come Prepared for Your Classes

Many students simply don't realize that being prepared makes a world of difference in what they learn from a class. Going to class without the supplies you need is like trying to play baseball without a glove. You just can't play the game right. Going without your assignments completed can be compared to trying to run a marathon without any preparation. You won't accomplish much.

Having your supplies is important

Have you ever found yourself in geometry class without your protractor or in English without your textbook? You are not alone. The problem of not having the necessary supplies for class is a common one for students. It is a simple problem that you can eliminate by putting a checklist on the front of each of your class notebooks or on the front of your assignment notebook or even on your locker door. Then all you have to do to be perfectly equipped is look over your checklist before you leave home or your locker for classes. You may find it helpful to use a checklist like the following or create a new one that fits your needs better.

Name of class:

_____ have completed assignment

_____ have textbook

_____ have notebook

_____ have workbook or lab manual

_____ have sharpened pencils

_____ have pens

_____ have other needed supplies:

_____ _____

_____ _____

_____ _____

Your assignments need to be completed

Notice that the number one priority on the checklist is to have your assignment completed. What this really means is, Are you ready to learn? If you haven't done the background reading, your participation in the class discussion will be limited. If you haven't done the written assignment, you will be playing catch-up for the entire class period. Furthermore, the teacher will quickly see you are unprepared for class.

It is important to realize that teachers make assignments for a reason—not just to keep you busy. Assignments give you the opportunity to practice the skills that you are learning in class, especially in English, foreign language, and math classes. They help you develop the skills that you will need in college and your career. Assignments also let you learn new material through your textbooks and prepare you to participate in class discussions. Assignments allow you to complete work that you began in class. Furthermore, they help you review what you have been learning in your classes.

Completing assignments helps you develop the good study habits that you will need in college. Go through the following assignment preparation checklist.

Assignment Preparation Checklist

1. Do you try to do all your assignments at the same time every day?   Yes   No

2. Do you keep an assignment notebook?   Yes   No

3. Do you review or work ahead on days when you don't have any assigned homework?   Yes   No

4. Do you make a list of questions about concepts or ideas that you do not understand in your assignments?   Yes   No

5. Do you keep a calendar that shows when future assignments are due?   Yes   No

6. Do you get help when you are having trouble with an assignment?   Yes   No

If you answered "No" to any of the questions on the checklist, set some goals now to improve those areas and keep a record of your progress on the following chart:

Today's date: _____

Assignment preparation goal 1: _____

_____

_____

_____

Date in four weeks: _____

Improvement noted: _____

_____

_____

_____

Today's date: _____

Assignment preparation goal 2: _____

_____

_____

_____

Date in four weeks: _____

Improvement noted: _____

_____

_____

_____

Choose a Good Seat

This section's heading may be making you laugh even before you begin to read about why this heading is necessary. First, answer this question: Where do you sit in a class when you are given this choice?

1. Do you try to sit in the back of the room?   Yes   No

2. Do you try to sit in the middle of the room?   Yes   No

3. Do you try to sit in the front of the room?   Yes   No

You are on the right track if you answered "Yes" to question number three. The very best seats in any classroom are the ones in the front row. By sitting in the front row or as close to the front as possible, you eliminate many of the distractions that can tear your concentration away from the classwork. You don't have to watch what other students are doing. You can see the teacher and the work that is done on the blackboard. Because you are so visible to the teacher, you are inclined to concentrate more on the lesson. In addition, you may have a chance for more casual conversation with the teacher.

Many students feel more comfortable and secure sitting farther back in a classroom. It requires some courage to sit up front. You are called on more often by the teacher so you need to be prepared. You never have the chance to take a quick nap or even daydream for a few minutes. However, since you are in a class to learn, it makes sense to choose a seat that gives you the best opportunity to learn. If you have never tried sitting in the front of a classroom, try it. You may be surprised to find out that where you sit can make a difference.

Participate for Success

By now you should know that what you say in class does make a difference. It is so important that some teachers in high school and even in college give a grade for class participation. But participation is more than winning "brownie" points with your teachers. It is being actively involved in the learning process. If you don't participate, you are rather like a sponge expecting to absorb learning simply because you are there. To participate simply, you need to be prepared, which helps you learn. There is also an interesting benefit to participation. By participating in a class you become interested in what you are learning and more eager to study.

Check your classroom participation. Answer the following questions to determine how well you are participating in your classes right now.

1. Do I have a good attendance record?   Yes   No

2. Do I pay attention to what is being said?   Yes   No

3. Do I take notes on class discussions?   Yes   No

4. Am I usually prepared to participate in class discussions?   Yes   No

5. Do I answer questions willingly?   Yes   No

6. Are my contributions valuable?   Yes   No

Any "No" answers indicate areas in which you should improve. Since both you and your classmates are enriched when you participate in class discussions, you should set some goals to improve your participation.

Today's date: _____

Participation goal 1: _____

_____

_____

_____

_____

Date in four weeks: _____

Improvement noted: _____

_____

_____

_____

_____

Today's date: _____

Participation goal 2: _____

_____

_____

_____

_____

Date in four weeks: _____

Improvement noted: _____

_____

_____

_____

Preparing to participate in class. Some students do not participate in class because they are afraid or too nervous to do so. Since most discussions are about the textbook, you can anticipate what one or two of the class discussion questions will be and practice answering them aloud. In fact, all students can improve their discussion skills by practicing the answers aloud to some of their SQ3R questions or end-of-the-chapter questions. Preparation for class discussions means having all the assignments done before class. It also means thinking of questions that will expand the discussion.

Become a Good Listener

You hear with your ears, but do you know how to listen? Listen and learn. Almost everything that you find on tests has been mentioned in class discussions and your teachers' lectures. If you listen carefully and jot down notes on what your teachers say, learning is much easier. It is important to learn how to listen in the classroom now, for in college many of your classes will be lectures. Answer the following questions to determine if you know how to listen and learn in the classroom:

	Always	Sometimes	Never
1. Do I think about what I am hearing during class?	_____	_____	_____
2. Do I stop listening when something is said that I find upsetting?	_____	_____	_____
3. Do I listen for important points?	_____	_____	_____
4. Do I listen for clues that suggest a major point is about to be made?	_____	_____	_____
5. Do I let my mind drift instead of listening?	_____	_____	_____
6. Am I easily distracted by other students?	_____	_____	_____

Work on improving your listening skills by making goals for all your "Never" answers.

Today's date: _____

Listening skills goal 1: _____

_____

_____

_____

Date in four weeks: _____

Improvement noted: _____

_____

_____

_____

_____

Today's date: _____

Listening skills goal 2: _____

_____

_____

_____

Date in four weeks: _____

Improvement noted: _____

_____

_____

_____

_____

Becoming a better listener

Distractions affect your listening. The farther back you sit, the more distractions there will be competing with the speaker. The average person speaks at a rate of approximately 125 words a minute. Yet your listening power is much greater. That is why you have to make sure your mind is on track and not racing ahead or wandering miles off course in the wrong direction while the speaker just seems to be rambling along. Increase your attention by taking the following steps to become an active listener:

- Take notes about what is being said.

- Write down questions to ask later.

- Look for the speaker's most important ideas.

- Relate what you are hearing to information that you already have.

- Think about what the speaker is saying.

Use clues. Look at the following list of phrases that teachers use to indicate that what they are going to say next is important. Then add to the list the clues that your teachers use. Get in the habit of paying attention when you hear these clues:

Listen carefully to this point.   I want to emphasize . . .

You should know the
reasons . . .   The major cause was . . .

_____   _____

_____   _____

Take Notes in Class

Taking good class notes is important in high school, and it is absolutely essential in college. In high school these notes help you remember what was discussed in class, give you useful explanations, help you recall the important things your teacher said, and supplement the material in your textbook. In college, these notes may be the major source of your information.

It is much easier to take notes on textbook materials than it is to take notes in class. When you take textbook notes, you always have the opportunity to go back and reread the material. There are few second chances when you are taking notes in class. You must listen attentively. Then you have to choose what is important and organize those facts in your mind as you are writing them down in your own words.

Don't make the mistake of trying to copy down every word that your teacher is saying. Learn to be selective and jot down only the important points. Be sure to write down all terms and definitions that are mentioned and anything that is ever written on the blackboard. You will find it helpful to take your notes in an outline form if your teachers present the material to you in an organized fashion.

Students who worry about having perfect notes are missing the boat. Write them as neatly as you can because it is a waste of time to recopy them. But during class just write your notes, then—as soon as possible after class—reread your notes to check for completeness and accuracy. After reviewing your notes, you may find it helpful to write a summary of them or to underline the important points.

Remember, lecture notes are not a substitute for reading your textbook. When lecturing, teachers usually give only a condensed version of what you will read in the textbook. One advantage of having lecture notes is that teachers often explain difficult textbook material during their lectures.

Develop Solid Relationships with Your Teachers

Teachers have the job of teaching, but learning is your job. Both jobs are much easier if you and your teachers work together. Your attitude plays a big role in the success of this partnership. Teachers know the students who don't care enough to arrive at class on time. They also notice students who start packing up early. They see the students who yawn and take catnaps. Teachers are also aware of students doing other assignments, writing notes, and whispering with their friends. Some teachers correct you; others do not. But all know that your behavior shows your attitude toward learning. They know whether you consider the classroom a social scene or a learning experience.

Talk to your teachers

You will not always understand everything that is being taught in your classes. However, you need to stay on top of the situation and get help quickly when you don't understand something, as most problems get larger—not smaller. Seek help from your teachers. They want you to succeed and can often help you turn things around in one brief meeting. Don't just talk to your teachers about academic problems; also talk to them about what interests you in their classes.

How do your teachers see you?

One step involved in applying to many colleges is getting recommendations from your teachers. Recommendation forms often ask teachers to fill out checklists comparing a student to other college-bound students. Fill out the Student Evaluation Checklist as you think your teachers would. It will give you a good idea of your strengths and weaknesses.

Student Evaluation Checklist

	Below average	Average	Good	Excellent	Outstanding
Punctuality					
Attendance					
Class participation					
Eagerness to learn					
Preparation for class					
Respect for teachers					
Respect for peers					
Intellectual curiosity					
Creativity					
Emotional maturity					
Personal initiative					
Energy					
Reaction to setbacks					

Become a
Better Reader

Are you currently racing or inching your way slowly through your reading assignments at school? Much of your success in school now and in college depends on your ability to read well.

You may think that your high school work requires a lot of reading, but it is just a fraction of what you will do in college. In majors like history, English, economics, psychology, and political science all of your classes will require vast amounts of reading. In fact, only a few majors in college do not require considerable reading. In this chapter, you will learn about ways to improve your reading skills and the importance of setting up a reading program to prepare yourself for college admissions tests and courses.

Test How Much You Know About Reading

Have you ever wondered exactly how much you know about reading? Test yourself right now by deciding whether the following statements are true or false.

1. It is impossible to improve your reading rate.	True	False
2. An average reader reads more than 400 words per minute.	True	False
3. Word-by-word reading does not affect your reading comprehension.	True	False
4. Your eye movements have nothing to do with your reading speed.	True	False
5. Skimming and scanning are the same skill.	True	False
6. Your vocabulary is not related to your reading comprehension.	True	False
7. As long as you know the main idea, you don't need to worry about the details.	True	False
8. Conclusions are always drawn for you in all your reading material.	True	False
9. The faster you read, the lower your comprehension is.	True	False
10. The faster you read, the less you appreciate what you have read.	True	False

If you are knowledgeable about reading, you know that every statement is false. Continue reading to learn how to improve your reading skills.

Banish Bad Reading Habits

If you understand what you have read in this book so far, you have basic reading skills that will allow you to survive in high school and college. However, you may have some bad habits that are keeping you from being a really good reader. Complete the following statements to find out more about your reading habits:

	Always	Sometimes	Never	
1. I	_____	_____	_____	read out loud to myself as I read.
2. I	_____	_____	_____	read at the same speed on all materials.
3. I	_____	_____	_____	backtrack over the material I have just read.
4. I	_____	_____	_____	use my finger or a pencil to point as I read.
5. I	_____	_____	_____	read one word at a time.
6. I	_____	_____	_____	have difficulty recognizing unfamiliar words.

Any statements that you completed with "Always" or "Sometimes" indicate bad reading habits. Continue reading to find out more about these bad habits and how to eliminate them before setting some new goals to improve your reading.

Reading out loud. Check that you are not also reading out loud when you read silently. Put your fingers over your lips right now as you are reading to see if you are moving them. Then put your fingers on your throat to see if you can feel any movement there. If you feel any movement in either place, it is a sign that you are saying words to yourself as you read. This habit slows down your reading because you can read much faster than you speak.

To correct any lip movement, try holding a pencil tightly between your lips as you read. If you have movement in your throat, you should try chewing gum, eating, or sucking on something while reading.

Reading at a single speed. You need more than one reading speed. You should race through light reading and slow down on new textbook material that you are trying to learn. Consider your purpose when reading and then adjust your speed. Practice adjusting your speed by reading materials that require different speeds like a dictionary, a textbook, and newspaper comic strips.

Backtracking. Some students can scarcely read a line without going back once or twice to read a word again. You can stop backtracking by forcing your eyes to keep moving along a line. Use a card to cover what you have just read so it is impossible for you to backtrack.

Pointing. Using an object to point to the words as you read slows down your reading speed. You can break this habit by placing a blank card or ruler under what you are reading.

Reading one word at a time. You read too slowly and don't make much sense out of what you are reading unless you read groups of words. To stop reading one word at a time, force yourself to read groups of words. You can make flash cards with simple phrases on them, and you can read out loud with a good reader, trying to copy the good reader's phrasing.

Not recognizing unfamiliar words. If too many words are unfamiliar when you are reading, you need to increase your vocabulary. Before reading textbook materials, study the word lists. Then look up unfamiliar words in the glossary so you know you how to pronounce them and what they mean. Be sure to say the words so you become accustomed to using them. You will find many additional vocabulary-building secrets in the next chapter.

Start to improve your reading skills by setting goals to eliminate your bad reading habits. You should notice improvement right away. Keep track of your progress on the following chart:

Today's date: _____

Reading goal 1: _____

_____

_____

_____

Date in four weeks: _____

Improvement noted: _____

_____

_____

_____

Today's date: _____

Reading goal 2: _____

_____

_____

_____

Date in four weeks: _____

Improvement noted: _____

_____

_____

_____

If you are not satisfied with your progress, you may need to take a reading course in high school. Such a course can make your high school and college work much easier.

Speed Up Your Reading

Do you ever run out of study time and still have more reading assignments to finish? Perhaps you are reading too slowly. Do you think that you are reading as fast as you can? If you think you are, you are probably wrong because almost anyone can read faster. Eliminating bad reading habits is a first step in increasing your reading speed. The second step is simply practicing reading faster for short periods of time.

Find out exactly what your reading rate is now by timing yourself as you read the following 900-word passage on franchising and fast foods. Before you start reading, make sure that you are in a comfortable place, preferably your own study area, and that you have eliminated all distractions. When you finish, you will be given the formula for calculating your reading rate. Begin by writing down the starting time in minutes and seconds or use a stopwatch.

Starting time: _____

Franchising and Fast Foods

You may have heard the word *franchising* before, but do you really know what the word means? Franchising is a method of distributing products or services. It is the method used by fast food chains like McDonald's, KFC, Pizza Hut, Wendy's, and Burger King to increase their growth. However, not only do established fast food companies use franchising as a way to grow, but new fast food companies like Boston Chicken and TCBY use franchising to make it in today's highly competitive fast food industry.

In franchising, there are two groups involved. The International Franchise Association (IFA) describes them as the *franchisor*, who lends a trademark, a trade name, and a business system, and the *franchisee*, who wants to open the new unit. The franchisee pays a royalty and often an initial fee for the right to do business under the franchisor's name and system. According to the IFA, the contract binding the franchisor and the franchisee is technically the *franchise*, but that term is often used to mean the actual business that the franchisee buys from the franchisor.

Fast food units can either be owned by the franchisor or the franchisee, and usually it is impossible to tell which is the case just by walking in the door of a restaurant. Whether you eat at a Wendy's that is owned by the company or one owned by a franchisee, the products, services, and quality should be the same.

When you buy a franchise, you are buying the name, the company's proven system for success, and its support, not only in getting your unit open but also in handling any difficulties that you may encounter in doing business. The franchisor gives one-on-one help in such areas as advertising, purchasing, inventory control, and personnel management. However, successful franchising is neither automatic nor easy. Franchising takes a great deal of planning and skill along with considerable financial risk.

Many fast food franchisors assist the franchisee in obtaining a credit line, negotiating a lease, and receiving consent from zoning and planning boards. Fast food franchisors also provide franchisees with operations manuals. In addition, franchisors usually run training schools that franchisees are required to attend. Fast food franchisors also provide franchisees with manuals that contain records of the initial training procedures for all phases of management and recipes to be updated as methods change.

Burger King requires its franchisees to attend a training center where for seven weeks they learn cooking, personnel supervision, and selection and bookkeeping. Dairy Queen holds a two-week training course for new franchisees where they spend time working in an actual store, learning how to make products and operate a store. Then an opening team spends three weeks with franchisees to help them open their stores. The team assists in all areas—from working with financial forms to interviewing and training employees.

Franchisees must conduct their new businesses according to stipulations outlined by the franchisors in contracts. These stipulations encompass a broad range of franchise activities including determining the precise amount of meat and spices to put in a hamburger, the correct amount of time for cooking a hamburger, and the menu items to sell. The contract also deals with other matters like hours of operation, inventory, insurance, personnel, and accounting. By establishing stipulations in the contract, a franchisor is able to control costs and, more importantly, promote a unified brand image of identical outlets throughout a wide area.

When the franchise agreement is signed, both the franchisor and the franchisee enter into a long-term relationship of perhaps as long as twenty years which may include an option to renew and extend the agreement. During that time, the franchisor sends district managers and inspectors regularly to visit the operating unit. This field service provides advice and assistance to the franchisee on daily operations, checks on the quality of the product and service, monitors the performance of the enterprise, and enforces regulations if necessary.

You can't just buy a franchise. There is a waiting list to become a franchisee at some of the chains. In fact, some people wait several years. Then there is the matter of money. What fast food franchises cost varies enormously. You can expect to need start-up capital of approximately $40,000 to more than $400,000, and these figures do not include the land, the building, or the cost of improving a site, which could run from over $100,000 to as much as $1 million. Some franchisors require their franchisees to have a financial worth of at least $250,000 and ready cash of $200,000 or more. Although it may sound like setting up a franchise is impossible. Start-up costs can be reduced substantially through leasing the land and/or building. In addition, some fast food chains help their long-time employees obtain their own franchises by providing them with low-interest loans and often by leasing buildings to them. An employee getting a franchise this way may only need as little as $50,000, which can be spent on start-up costs.

Although becoming a franchisee may appeal to you, you must also consider the disadvantages. The firm imposes strict controls. Quality of the product is regulated, and a large capital investment is required.

Stopping time: _____

Determine how fast you read

To find out exactly what your reading rate was, subtract your starting time from your stopping time or use your stopwatch time. Reading time: _____

Next, change your total reading time into seconds. Seconds: _____

Then divide the 868 words in the passage by your total reading time in seconds to get your reading rate per second. Reading rate per second: _____

The last step is to multiply your reading rate in seconds by 60 to get your reading rate in words per minute. Words per minute rate: _____

Most high school students should read a passage like the one you just read at a rate of between 200 and 300 words per minute. Your speed should drop below 150 words per minute on very technical material. When you are reading for relaxation, your speed should accelerate. Reading experts believe that 800 words a minute is as fast as anyone can read material with comprehension.

Practice to improve your reading speed

With practice, you can improve your speed, but you must be careful not to sacrifice understanding to get speed. Practice on a variety of materials. Read just two pages a day as fast as you can for a week, and you will begin to notice some improvement. Keep practicing, and your rate will keep improving. Remember to adjust your speed to suit the material. Keep track of your improvement on the Reading Speed chart.

Reading Speed
(words per minute)

Date	Pleasure reading	Textbook reading

Move your eyes more efficiently

Try watching people's eyes as they read. Their eyes don't just glide smoothly across a page—they pause and then move on. When their eyes pause, they are reading. That pause is called a *fixation*, and if you can decrease the number of fixations that your eyes make, you can increase your speed.

The number of fixations that people make in reading a line is related to how much they see at each pause. So to reduce fixations, it is necessary to increase how much is seen in each pause. One way to practice doing this is to run your finger down the middle of a page and see how much you can see on either side of it. You can do the same thing by drawing a line down the center of a reading passage.

Learn to Skim and Scan Material

It seems like students have more to read every year they spend in school. So you have to be smart and know when you need to read every word and when it is sufficient to read just a few words here and there in a passage. After all, you don't read the entire telephone book when you look up a friend's phone number. In the same way, you shouldn't read the entire Constitution when you only need to know what the Twenty-fifth Amendment is. Skimming and scanning are the two skills that you use when it is not necessary or desirable to carefully read every word in a passage. While these skills are extremely helpful in high school, they are absolutely essential in college.

Skimming gives you the picture

Survey is the first step in the SQ3R method. When you survey a textbook, you are skimming. You are just reading enough to get the general idea of what the material is about. In many cases, that means just reading the headings. You should do considerable skimming when you are doing research for reports and term papers. This means quickly glancing through an encyclopedia article on Harry Truman or automobiles, for example, to sense what information is given or thumbing through a book to see what topics are covered.

To skim, read only headings, words in boldface or italic type, topic sentences, and paragraphs that grab your interest. Remember, you are not looking for anything specific. You are only trying to get an overview.

Scanning helps you find specifics

In scanning, like in skimming, your eyes must move quickly over the printed page. However, when you scan you know specifically what you are looking for, so your eyes ignore most of the words as you search for a key word or phrase. Use scanning to find words like *Stamp Act, stamen,* and *ion* in your textbooks. Be sure to scan the next time you are trying to find a name or date in your social studies textbook.

Understand What You Read

It is essential to be able to read fast enough to get through all your assignments each day. However, if you don't remember or understand what you read, your speed is not important. Testing your comprehension is not quite as easy as finding out your reading speed because there are five different skills that you must have to truly understand what you read.

Read the following passage. Then answer the questions that follow. Each question tests a different comprehension skill.

History of Fast Food

The history of fast food restaurants from the first restaurant to the thousands that exist today is quite short because the fast food concept is new. However, it has not taken long for fast food restaurants to become a dynamic part of the food service industry.

People are intrigued with the speed and assembly-line efficiency with which meals are prepared in these restaurants, and this has kept them coming back. They like the way the fast food industry has always tried to serve food to its customers quickly, efficiently, and economically. Much may have changed since the first fast food restaurants were started, but these characteristics have never changed.

The first European settlers in the United States wanted quick, inexpensive meals, but there were few places to get them. Taverns were about the only spots where people could go to get a quick bite to eat, and free food was served occasionally to those who purchased drinks.

More than a hundred years later came a great new invention that offered fast food service—the lunch wagon. These horse-drawn wagons sold sandwiches, slices of pie, and drinks around the clock in front of factories, parks, theaters, and other places where large crowds of people gathered. Over time, these wagons became larger and larger, and soon they were big enough for customers to step inside them out of the wind and rain to order their food. In fact, some of these wagons even had places for customers to sit. It was not long before these wagons stopped traveling and parked in single spots.

After the Civil War, drugstores began serving a new drink made out of sweet syrup and soda water. This drink became even more popular when someone thought of adding ice cream to it. Ice cream sodas became so well liked that most drugstores soon had soda fountains to serve them. Before long, soda fountains started adding different fast food items to their menus.

By the 1920s, many soda fountains had turned into luncheonettes, and coffee shops became popular. People had many different places that served food faster than traditional restaurants. They could grab a sandwich as they passed a lunch wagon or sit on a stool and be served quickly at a soda fountain, luncheonette, or coffee shop. But even these restaurants did not satisfy people's demand for fast food service, so cafeterias and other restaurants where people were willing to serve themselves emerged.

1. Main idea: What is this passage about?

_____

_____

_____

_____

2. Details: How did drugstores change after the Civil War?

_____

_____

_____

_____

3. Sequence: Were taverns or drugstores the first places to serve food quickly?

_____

_____

_____

_____

4. Drawing conclusions: Why has the fast food industry continued to grow?

_____

_____

_____

_____

_____

5. Vocabulary: What does the word *efficiency* mean?

_____

_____

_____

_____

_____

You will find the answers to these questions as you read more about the different comprehension skills. In high school it is often most important to remember details for tests, but in college, besides knowing details, you have to know the main idea and be able to draw conclusions. Knowing vocabulary is always essential to comprehension. Being able to sequence helps you organize information in your mind. When you take college entrance tests, you will have questions like the ones you just answered that require you to use all the comprehension skills.

Finding the main idea

The passage you read was about the emergence of different kinds of fast food restaurants. In informational material, like this passage, authors use headings, introductory statements, and summaries to emphasize the main idea. Both the title and the introductory paragraph gave you the main idea of this passage on the history of fast food.

In textbooks, each paragraph has a main idea that is usually stated in a topic sentence. The topic is frequently found in the first sentence, but it can be anywhere in the paragraph. Some paragraphs don't have topic sentences. Then you have to generalize the main idea from reading the entire paragraph. Once you train yourself to pick out the topic sentence or main idea of a paragraph, your comprehension will improve.

Write down the main idea of the proceeding paragraph.

Main idea: _____

_____

_____

_____

_____

The main idea was stated in the first sentence, which was the topic sentence of the paragraph. Read the next paragraph on recalling details and try to pick out the topic sentence.

Topic sentence: _____

_____

_____

Recalling details

Main ideas are important when you are studying, but to really learn a subject you need to remember details. For example, it is helpful to know the main idea of the passage on the history of fast food, but you won't really know much about that topic unless you know details about the taverns, lunch wagons, drugstores, and other places where food was served quickly. The answer to the question you were asked required knowing more details about drugstores. The answer was that drugstores started serving a new drink.

You will find it helpful to remember details in relation to the main idea rather than in isolation. Read the next paragraph for details. Then note how they relate to the main idea.

There are job openings in the fast food industry at all levels. Everyone has heard about the shortage of workers for entry-level positions. There is also an excellent opportunity for people to become restaurant managers. If you choose to have a career in fast food, your chances for advancement are excellent. All this makes for a rosy job picture.

Main idea: _____

_____

_____

_____

_____

Related details: _____

_____

_____

_____

_____

_____

Following sequence

You won't really understand the passage on the history of fast food unless you know the order in which different kinds of fast food places emerged. You should know that taverns served fast food before drugstores. Sequencing is an important part of reading comprehension. You obviously need to know the order or sequence of events in history. But you also need to know the sequence of events in novels for your English class and in experiments in your science class.

You can improve your sequencing skills by getting in the habit of writing down or retelling events in the order in which they occurred. Note how easy it would be to remember the order of the emergence of fast food places by completing this list.

1. taverns

2. _____

3. _____

4. luncheonettes

5. _____

6. cafeterias

Drawing conclusions

As you study, you have probably noticed that textbook authors usually sum up each chapter. They draw conclusions for you. However, you read other materials like the "History of Fast Food" for which you need to come to your own conclusions. You were asked why the fast food industry has continued to grow. After thinking about the information you were given, you should be able to come to the conclusion that the industry continues to grow because people want food that can be served fast.

Mastering vocabulary

If you cannot understand key words when you are reading, you will have difficulty understanding what you are reading. Often words are defined in text or you can guess what they mean because they are related to words you know. You were asked to define *efficiency*. This isn't too difficult because it is related to *efficient,* so you can determine that it means the quality of being efficient. And *efficient* means capable of producing a result without causing any waste. The best way to increase your vocabulary is to read. In the next chapter, you will read about more ways to improve your vocabulary.

Working on your comprehension skills

You must understand what you read. If you can't answer "Yes" to all of the following questions, you need to set goals to improve your comprehension skills:

1. Can you recognize topic sentences?   Yes   No

2. Do you usually understand the main idea
   of a reading passage?   Yes   No

3. Are you able to recall details easily?   Yes   No

4. Can you retell the sequence of a series of
   events that you have read about?   Yes   No

5. Do you usually draw the correct conclusions
   from reading a passage?   Yes   No

6. Do you recognize most of the words in your reading assignments?   Yes   No

7. Do you usually understand what you read?   Yes   No

Today's date: _____

Comprehension goal 1: _____

_____

_____

_____

_____

Date in four weeks: _____

Improvement noted: _____

_____

_____

_____

_____

Today's date: _____

Comprehension goal 2: _____

_____

_____

_____

_____

Date in four weeks: _____

Improvement noted: _____

_____

_____

_____

_____

Establish a Reading Program

One of the best ways to prepare for college is to read—not just your school assignments but classic literary works. If you know what college you are planning to attend, write to ask the English department for a suggested reading list. You can also obtain good lists designed to help you prepare for college from your high school English teachers or librarian. Remember that new books are always appearing on the market, so you will want to update any list that is more than three years old.

If you want to get started right now, you can use the following list that has been compiled from the lists of several colleges. First, read through the list and check off the books you have read. Second, talk with friends, your parents, and teachers about which books on the list would be the best ones for you to read first. Circle these books and make it a habit to use them for book reports. Third, establish a reading program. Set aside fifteen to thirty minutes each day for reading and enter that time on your personal study schedule. Such a program will be very effective in improving your reading skills, increasing your vocabulary, broadening your general knowledge, and preparing you for college admissions tests.

_____ Aesop, fables

_____ Agee, James, *A Death in the Family*

_____ Alcott, Louisa May, *Little Women*

_____ Anderson, Sherwood, *Winesburg, Ohio*

_____ Auden, W. H., poetry

_____ Austen, Jane, *Pride and Prejudice*

_____ Baldwin, James, *Go Tell It on the Mountain*

_____ Beckett, Samuel, *Waiting for Godot*

_____ The Bible

_____ Bronte, Charlotte, *Jane Eyre*

_____ Bronte, Emily, *Wuthering Heights*

_____ Browning, Elizabeth B., poetry

_____ Browning, Robert, poetry

_____ Bunyan, John, *Pilgrim's Progress*

_____ Camus, Albert, *The Stranger*

_____ Carroll, Lewis, *Alice in Wonderland*

_____ Cather, Willa, *My Antonia*

_____ Chaucer, Geoffrey, *The Canterbury Tales*

_____ Chekhov, Anton, *The Cherry Orchard*

_____ Conrad, Joseph, *Heart of Darkness; Lord Jim*

_____ Crane, Stephen, *The Red Badge of Courage*

_____ de Cervantes, Miguel, *Don Quixote*

_____ Defoe, Daniel, *The Adventures of Robinson Crusoe*

_____ Dickens, Charles, *A Tale of Two Cities; David Copperfield; Oliver Twist; Great Expectations*

_____ Dostoevsky, Fyodor, *The Brothers Karamazov; Crime and Punishment*

_____ Doyle, Sir Arthur Conan, *Adventures of Sherlock Holmes*

_____ Dreiser, Theodore, *An American Tragedy*

_____ Eliot, George, *Silas Marner*

_____ Ellison, Ralph, *Invisible Man*

_____ Emerson, Ralph Waldo, essays

_____ Faulkner, William, *Light in August*

_____ Fermi, Enrico, *Atoms in the Family*

_____ Fielding, Henry, *Tom Jones*

_____ Fitzgerald, F. Scott, *The Great Gatsby*

_____ Forster, E. M., *A Passage to India*

_____ Frank, Anne, *Diary of a Young Girl*

_____ Frost, Robert, poetry

_____ Golding, William, *Lord of the Flies*

_____ Greene, Graham, *The Power and the Glory*

_____ Hamilton, Edith, *Mythology*

_____ Hawthorne, Nathaniel, *House of the Seven Gables; The Scarlet Letter*

_____ Heller, Joseph, *Catch-22*

_____ Hemingway, Ernest, *A Farewell to Arms; For Whom the Bell Tolls; The Old Man and the Sea*

_____ Homer, *The Odyssey; The Iliad*

_____ Hugo, Victor, *The Hunchback of Notre Dame*

_____ Ibsen, Henrik, *A Doll's House*

_____ James, Henry, *The American; The Turn of the Screw*

_____ Kafka, Franz, *The Trial*

_____ Kipling, Rudyard, *The Jungle Books*

_____ Lawrence, D. H., *Sons and Lovers; Women in Love*

_____ Lee, Harper, *To Kill a Mockingbird*

_____ Lewis, Sinclair, *Babbitt; Main Street*

_____ London, Jack, *The Call of the Wild*

_____ Mailer, Norman, *The Naked and the Dead*

_____ Mann, Thomas, *The Magic Mountain*

_____ Marquand, John P., *Point of No Return*

_____ Melville, Herman, *Moby Dick*

_____ Miller, Arthur, *Death of a Salesman*

_____ Mitchell, Margaret, *Gone with the Wind*

_____ O'Neill, Eugene, *The Emperor Jones*

_____ Orwell, George, *Animal Farm; 1984*

_____ Ovid, *Metamorphoses*

_____ Parkman, Francis, *The Oregon Trail*

_____ Pasternak, Boris, *Dr. Zhivago*

_____ Paton, Alan, *Cry, the Beloved Country*

_____ Poe, Edgar Allan, tales and poems

_____ Porter, William Sydney (O. Henry), tales

_____ Remarque, Erich Maria, *All Quiet on the Western Front*

_____ Roberts, Kenneth, *Robin Hood Tales*

_____ Rolvaag, Ole Edvart, *Giants in the Earth*

_____ Salinger, J. D., *The Catcher in the Rye*

_____ Sandburg, Carl, *Abraham Lincoln;* poetry

_____ Scott, Sir Walter, *Ivanhoe*

_____ Shakespeare, William, *Hamlet; The Merchant of Venice; Julius Caesar; Macbeth; Romeo and Juliet*

_____ Shaw, George Bernard, *Pygmalion*

_____ Shelley, Mary, *Frankenstein*

_____ Sophocles, *Oedipus Rex*

_____ Steinbeck, John, *Of Mice and Men; The Grapes of Wrath*

_____ Stevenson, Robert Louis, *Dr. Jekyll and Mr. Hyde; Treasure Island*

_____ Stowe, Harriet Beecher, *Uncle Tom's Cabin*

_____ Swift, Jonathan, *Gulliver's Travels*

_____ Thackeray, William Makepeace, *Vanity Fair*

_____ Thoreau, Henry David, *Walden*

_____ Thurber, James, *The Thurber Carnival*

_____ Tolkien, J. R. R., *Lord of the Rings*

_____ Tolstoy, Leo, *War and Peace*

_____ Twain, Mark, *The Adventures of Huckleberry Finn; The Adventures of Tom Sawyer*

_____ Verne, Jules, *Around the World in 80 Days*

_____ Wells, H. G., *The Time Machine*

_____ Wharton, Edith, *The Age of Innocence; Ethan Frome*

_____ Wilder, Thornton, *Our Town*

_____ Williams, Tennessee, *A Streetcar Named Desire*

_____ Woolf, Virginia, *To the Lighthouse*

_____ Wouk, Herman, *The Caine Mutiny*

_____ Wright, Richard, *Black Boy; Native Son*

_____ Wyss, Johann David, *The Swiss Family Robinson*

Boost Your Skill Level **5**

You have probably heard the expression "Practice makes perfect" hundreds of times. And you have probably followed this dictate many times as you have learned to do such things as swim, drive a car, or play the piano. Your school skills are no different: The more you practice them, the better they will become.

When you work on your vocabulary, speaking, research, writing, spelling, and computer skills; not only do you boost your skill level, but you also make it much easier for yourself to handle high school. If you don't reach a certain level of competence in these very important skills, you may find it essential to spend time in college taking remedial classes to acquire them.

In this chapter, you will learn what you need to do to boost your vocabulary, speaking, research, writing, spelling, and computer skills.

Increasing Your Vocabulary

You will learn a few new words every year without any effort. But that kind of vocabulary growth is not sufficient to build the vocabulary you need during high school and for college and college admissions tests. At this point in your education, you have to make an active effort to learn new words. As you increase your vocabulary, you will also be improving your reading rate and comprehension.

Learning vocabulary for admissions tests

Begin working on your vocabulary now so you won't be disappointed when you see your scores on the verbal sections of college admissions tests. How many of the following words that have appeared on these tests do you know?

1. sophisticated	6. complacent
2. indigenous	7. gullible
3. clique	8. truculent
4. paean	9. embroil
5. meticulous	10. olfactory

Did you know all of these words? Were you interested enough to look up any of the ones you didn't know? You need to have an interest in words if you truly want to build your vocabulary. Use one of the tools mentioned in the next section to learn the words that you did not know.

Tools for building your vocabulary

There are familiar tools that will help you increase your vocabulary. It is now time to start using these tools.

Dictionary. Don't be a student who uses the dictionary only to look up the meanings of words and does not use information in entries about the pronunciation, synonyms, antonyms, parts of speech, or etymology of words. Become interested in the study of words, especially the history of words. Many English words come from other languages.

Thesaurus. Do you find yourself in the habit of using the same words over and over again? If so, you should be using a thesaurus, which is a book of synonyms, to expand your vocabulary. The thesaurus helps you replace overused words like *big* and *little* with more exciting words like *extensive, sizable, bantam,* and *petite. Use* your thesaurus to find substitutes for the following overused words.

good: _____ _____ _____

poor: _____ _____ _____

happy: _____ _____ _____

get: _____ _____ _____

Flash cards. Flash cards are the best tool that you can use to teach yourself new words. Just by making the flash card, you are imprinting the word on your brain. Write the word on one side of the card and the definition on the other side. Add a synonym and an antonym for the word, and you have a wealth of information on one card. Use flash cards with a study partner or use them alone.

Computer programs. Computer vocabulary programs are a new tool that can be used to increase your vocabulary. Not only will they let you track your progress in acquiring vocabulary, many also concentrate on tracking words commonly found in the verbal section of the SAT I.

Learning meaning from context clues

You will never get through your reading assignments if you need to look up a lot of words. Do you know the meanings of the words *heinous, perpetrated, atrocities, assimilate,* and *precipitated?* Read the following paragraph. You will encounter the words that have just been mentioned. See if you can get the meaning of each word from the words around it in the paragraph.

Many *heinous* crimes were perpetrated in Paris during the French Revolution. Greedy villains invaded the residences of the royal families, looting and committing *atrocities* against these defenseless citizens. Many of these royal citizens tried to *assimilate* themselves into the general population in hopes of escaping the spontaneous trials that *precipitated* death.

Now write the definition of the words. Use your dictionary if you need help.

heinous: _____

_____

_____

perpetrated: _____

_____

_____

atrocities: _____

_____

_____

assimilate: _____

_____

_____

precipitated: _____

_____

_____

Breaking down and multiplying words

Words come in parts—prefixes, roots, and suffixes. If you know the meanings of the parts, you may be able to figure out the meanings of the whole words. Learning the meanings of word parts is an easy way to increase your vocabulary.

Prefixes. Prefixes are the word parts that are found at the beginnings of words. They help you start unlocking the meanings of words. For example, the prefix *re-* means "again," so the word *reread* means "to read again." What do you think the words *reformulate, readmit,* and *reclassify* mean? Learn to recognize some of the more commonly used prefixes and memorize their definitions. Here is a list of prefixes that you should know:

- *trans-*: cross

- *hypo-*: under

- *pro*: forward

- *il*: not

- *co-*: with

- *mono-*: one

- *retro*: back

- *ex-*: out

- *bi-*: two

- *ad*: to

Suffixes. The word parts at the end of words are called *suffixes*. You probably know that the suffix *-less* means "without." If you add *-less* to the word *sense,* you form the word *senseless*, which means "without sense."

Look at the following list of common suffixes and their meanings and learn to recognize and use them to help you define unfamiliar words:

- *-able*: capable of being
- *-hood*: state of
- *-ness*: like
- *-ful*: full of

- *-ly*: in the manner of
- *-or*: person
- *-en*: make or become
- *-logy*: study of

Roots. A root is the basic part of a word. Prefixes and suffixes are added to roots. You can expand your vocabulary by memorizing frequently used roots that come from Latin and Greek. For example, *crat* comes from the Greek word for *rule* or *power.* Write down all the words that you know that have this root:

autocrat: _____

Compound words. Remember when in elementary school you had fun joining two words together to form a new word—such as dog + house = doghouse. See if you can join some of these words together to form compound words:

ad	slaughter	worthy	ship
fore	man	seer	partisan
over	close	here	note

_____   _____

_____   _____

_____   _____

Increasing your knowledge of words

The more you know about words, the more easily you will be able to build your vocabulary. Knowing the multiple meanings of a word as well as its synonyms and antonyms are helpful tools. For example, it's easier to learn a new word like *garrulous* if you know its synonyms is *talkative*.

Multiple meanings. You can hear the telephone *ring,* or you can wear a *ring.* Words with completely different meanings can be spelled the same. This can be confusing if you don't use context clues to know which meaning is intended. Can you think of another meaning for each of the following words?

reservation: keeping something back

reservation: _____

quail: a migratory game bird

quail: _____

fleet: a group of warships

fleet: _____

Synonyms. Synonyms are words that have the same or nearly the same meaning. They expand your vocabulary and make what you say more precise and more interesting. For example, a house can also be a *residence* or a *dwelling*. An *order* from a teacher should be obeyed; however, a *command* might be obeyed faster. Match each word in column 1 to its synonym in column 2:

_____	1. keen	a. appall	
_____	2. overcome	b. disparity	
_____	3. inequality	c. apex	
_____	4. pinnacle	d. sharp	
_____	5. dismay	e. conquer	

Answers: 1. d , 2. e, 3. b, 4. c, 5. a

Antonyms. These are words that are opposite in meaning, such as, *remain* and *depart* and *succeed* and *fail*. Can you match the following antonyms?

_____	1. robust	a. doe
_____	2. buck	b. masculine
_____	3. obese	c. apex
_____	4. feminine	d. skinny
_____	5. nadir	e. frail

Answers: 1. e, 2. a, 3. d, 4. b, 5. c

Building a good vocabulary

It helps to know about prefixes, suffixes, roots, synonyms, and antonyms, but the real secret is to read. The more you read, the more new words you will meet and learn from context clues. Read everything you can get your hands on—not just your textbooks. You should read magazines, the sports page, and as many books as you can from the suggested reading list in Chapter 4. If you don't read because you find reading too difficult, then you have to start reading material that is easier until you become a more skilled reader.

Becoming a Better Speaker

Every day in class you are probably expected to answer questions or participate in discussion. As a speaker, you have the job of sending a message to your listeners. First, you have to make sure that you are prepared and have a message to send. Second, you have to send the message in such a way that your listeners can receive it. Answer the following questions to see how you are doing as a speaker:

1. Do you monopolize classroom discussions?   Yes   No

2. Do you rarely speak in class?   Yes   No

3. Do you always take the position that you are right?   Yes   No

4. Are you always negative?   Yes   No

5. Do you frequently contradict others?   Yes   No

6. Do you interrupt when someone else is speaking?   Yes   No

7. Do you frequently try to change the topic of a discussion?   Yes   No

8. Do you give only one-word answers to questions?   Yes   No

9. Do you look at the floor, wall, or your desk when speaking in class?   Yes   No

10. Do you always mumble or speak too softly?   Yes   No

To be the best possible speaker in your high school and college classes, you need to answer "No" to these questions. Being aware of your speaking faults is the first step in correcting them. Then you need to make goals to improve your speaking skills.

Today's date: _____

Speaking goal 1: _____

_____

_____

_____

_____

Date in four weeks: _____

Improvement noted: _____

_____

_____

_____

_____

Today's date: _____

Speaking goal 2: _____

_____

_____

_____

_____

Date in four weeks: _____

Improvement noted: _____

_____

_____

_____

_____

How to ask questions

Participation in classroom discussions does not just mean answering questions. It also means asking them. You need to be curious enough about what you are studying to want more information and your classmates' and teachers' opinions. Skillful questioners know what types of questions to ask to get the answers they need. A general question like "What can I learn from reading this book?" will let the person answering give a very broad reply. If you want to get a more specific answer, you need to ask a limiting question like "Does this book have information about financial aid?" When you are trying to gather in-depth information about a certain subject, you need to ask probing questions such as "Why do you consider the person who wrote this book an expert on financial aid?"

You probably have a number of questions about the college admissions process. Try writing down questions now that will get you the answers you need. Then ask your counselor or college advisor for the answers.

General question: _____

_____

_____

_____

_____

Limiting questions: (1) _____

_____

_____

_____

_____

(2) _____

_____

_____

_____

_____

Probing questions: (1) _____

_____

_____

_____

_____

(2) _____

_____

_____

_____

_____

(3) _____

_____

_____

_____

_____

How to answer questions

To answer questions effectively, you have to know what you are talking about. You can't do this if you haven't done your assignments. You also have to know what is asked. This means you have to listen to a question in order to answer it. Before you begin to answer a question, make an outline in your mind in order to organize what you say. Keep in mind that once you start to talk what you say can never be erased. To improve your ability to answer questions, practice answering end-of-the-chapter questions aloud before class. You may find it helpful to do this in front of a mirror, or use a tape recorder to see how smoothly you answer questions.

How to handle oral reports

The most common kind of formal speech, outside of those practiced in speech class, is the oral report. What you are being asked to do is simply to give the same information that you would give in a written report. You need to have an introduction, a body, and a conclusion to your speech. Your topic should be narrow enough so that you can handle it in the few minutes you have to give your report. Like a written report, an oral report needs to be based on an outline. You can put the outline on note cards and use it when you are giving your speech. It is always better to give your report from a few note cards than from an entire written report. This eliminates the possibility of your reading instead of speaking to the class. When preparing an oral report, remember to organize your time so that you are able to practice it aloud several times.

Developing Your Research Skills

Do you know where to look for information on careers in public service or the basic rules of baseball? Most students find that research is the hardest part of writing any paper or preparing an oral report. Research involves knowing where and how to find information. This is one skill that you will use repeatedly in college.

The library is still the place where most high school students need to start their research. Even the smallest high school library is a vast storehouse of information. At the information desk of the library, you can usually obtain a pamphlet describing what material is available in the library and where it is located. You will not just find books but also have hands-on access to newspapers, magazines, reference books, government documents, films, videos, records, and much more. You will also be able to use a computer to access the vast amount of material on the Internet.

How to research in a library

You may not have a specific topic for a report or paper but want to explore material in the library on several topics before choosing one. Once you have selected a topic, you may find it necessary to narrow the topic even further after doing some research. It is often a good idea to read an article in an encyclopedia to get an overview of a topic before beginning any research. Where you begin your research depends on the timeliness of the topic. Research on current issues should begin with magazines, newspapers, the vertical file and the Internet, while research on less current topics can begin with books. As you become a more expert researcher, you will begin to use government documents, yearbooks, almanacs, and the wide array of indexes that help you find specialized information.

How to find a book

Whether you are doing research in your high school library or a college library, you follow exactly the same steps to find a book. You go to the computer catalog where all the books in the library are listed by title, author, and subject. At one time this information was stored on cards in drawers, but now it is usually stored in computers. You should be able to get a printout of all the information needed to find specific books on the shelf.

The Dewey Decimal System. The call number you find on the printout for a book, is also on the spine of the book. If a library uses the Dewey Decimal System, books will be numbered according to these classifications:

Numbers	Major divisions	Subdivisions
000–99	General Works	encyclopedias, bibliographies, periodicals
100–199	Philosophy	logic, psychology, religion
200–299	Religion	
300–399	Social Sciences	political science, economics, law, education, government
400–499	Language	dictionaries, grammars
500–599	Pure Science	mathematics, physics, astronomy, chemistry, biology
600–699	Technology	medicine, engineering, agriculture, business, radio, TV
700–799	The Arts	architecture, sculpture, painting, music, sports
800–899	Literature	novels, poetry, plays
900–999	History and Geography	

The Library of Congress System. Many large libraries use the Library of Congress Classification System. The books in this system are classified by twenty-one letters of the alphabet representing major subject areas.

A. General Works	N. Fine Arts
B. Philosophy, Psychology, and Religion	P. Language and Literature
C, D, E, F. History	Q. Science
G. Geography, Anthropology, and Recreation	R. Medicine
H. Social Sciences	S. Agriculture
J. Political Science	T. Technology
K. Law	U. Military Science
L. Education	V. Naval Science
M. Music	W. Bibliography and Library Science

Browsing. Once you have found a book on the library shelves, look at the other books next to it, as they are on related topics. You may find other books that you want to investigate further.

How to find a magazine article

In the past when students looked for articles in nontechnical magazines, they consulted the *Reader's Guide* in book form. While you can still find paper copies of the *Reader's Guide,* in most libraries the computer has become the tool for searching for magazine articles. Not only will the computer enable you to find information on articles in hundreds of magazines, but it may also print out the article for you, saving you the trouble of having to find a paper copy of it. In addition, on the computer there are abstracts of most articles, making it easy for you to determine which articles you want to see in their entirety. Libraries have access to databases beyond those concerning general interest publications that let you find full-text articles exploring social, scientific, historic, economic, political, and global issues in both domestic and international publications.

Specific subjects. Many students don't seem to know about the extraordinary number of magazines that are written on specific subjects. Information about these magazines will not always be found in computer databases at your library but can be found in specific subject index books like the following:

- *Current Index to Journals in Education*

- *Art Index*

- *The Music Index*

- *Biological and Agricultural Index*

- *Business Periodical Index*

How to find more information

Information in a library is not limited to books and magazines. The better you understand what other sources of information there are, the easier it will be for you to research. Spend time browsing through the reference section in a library until you become thoroughly acquainted with the following materials. It will make your research much easier. Don't ever forget to get help from librarians—they know how to research every subject.

Encyclopedias. Most students use general encyclopedias, which have information on just about everything. These books are now available on CD-ROM in many libraries.

There are also specialized encyclopedias on subjects such as the following:

- baseball

- wildlife

- education

- historic forts

- shells

- awards

Atlases. If you are looking for any type of map—physical, population, political—there are atlases that will provide this information.

Almanacs. When you want up-to-date facts and statistics about such topics as sports, well known people, world events, astronomical events, or ZIP codes, you will find them in almanacs, which are published once a year.

Handbooks. These books give an overview of one or more subjects and are arranged for quick location of facts. The title of a handbook, such as *The East European and Soviet Data Handbook*, usually indicates what material it covers.

Yearbooks. Put out each year, yearbooks give a summary of facts and statistics for the preceding year. Some yearbooks such as *Yearbook of the United Nations*, are limited to single subjects.

Bibliographies. These reference books help you find books in various subject areas, such as history or psychology. If you are unfamiliar with bibliographies, consult the *Guide to Reference Books,* which will help you locate reference books.

Newspapers. Most libraries have local newspapers as well as access on microfilm, microfiche, or the Internet to major newspapers like *The New York Times* or the *Wall Street Journal.*

How to research on the Internet

The Internet has become an important research tool. It is a gargantuan source of information from every country on earth. Your on-line research typically will begin with a search engine. Simply typing a term such as *bears* in the search engine search window can result in thousands of hits. You must learn how to use a site's research procedures in order to hone in on the material that you are seeking. Otherwise, you will have to go through scores of hits about bears, for example, to find relevant information about the Chicago Bears football team.

Research on the Internet is not limited to using search engines to find Web sites. You can seek answers from experts by sending them e-mail messages. For example, you can communicate with astronauts on space shuttle missions and climbers on Mt. Everest. You can post questions on electronic bulletin boards. You can visit the Web sites of newspapers and magazines. You can also enter chat rooms to talk about topics that you are researching. Books, magazines, newspapers, friends, family members, and teachers can also steer you to helpful Web sites that will make your research easier.

Caution: The Internet is full of sites with unreliable information. You must carefully consider the value of each source you use.

How good is a source?

You may find it difficult to decide which research sources to use.

Follow these guidelines when deciding which are the best sources:

1. Don't judge a book by its cover or a Web site by its appearance. Looks can deceive.

2. Find out the professional credentials of the author or creator of published or Internet materials.

3. Determine the date the information was created. The more current the material the better, unless you are researching the past.

4. Attempt to verify information, especially information that contradicts other material that you have identified.

Improving Your Writing Skills

Take courses that require you to write in high school, for in college your entire grade for a quarter or semester may depend on a paper or essays written on a final examination. When teachers return your written work, study the errors that you have made because these are the areas that require your attention. Now determine if you have mastered the skills essential to good writing:

1. Do you know how to make note cards?   Yes   No

2. Can you write a bibliography?   Yes   No

3. Do you choose narrow topics?   Yes   No

4. Can you outline a paper?   Yes   No

5. Do you know how to use good grammar?   Yes   No

6. Can you write an introduction, body, and
    conclusion for a paper?   Yes   No

7. Can you correctly cite the sources you have
    used in your papers?   Yes   No

If there are any areas in which you cannot confidently answer "Yes," you need to set goals for improvement.

Today's date: _____

Writing goal 1: _____

_____

_____

_____

Date in four weeks: _____

Improvement noted: _____

_____

_____

_____

_____

Today's date: _____

Writing goal 2: _____

_____

_____

_____

_____

Date in four weeks: _____

Improvement noted: _____

_____

_____

_____

The writing process

The moment you receive an assignment, organize your time. Too many students devote too much time to research and too little time to writing and editing. Before beginning to write, make an outline. This is an easy task when you use note cards. By simply sorting the cards into an appropriate order, you can create an outline.

When you write your first draft, you want to achieve a balance between writing so fast that your paper is full of errors and plodding so slowly that your paper loses all of its spontaneity. Proofreading is the vital process that makes every paper the best it can be. All students need to develop a list of questions to use as a guidepost for catching errors. Read the following first two paragraphs of the rough draft of a high school student's paper. You will note numerous errors. Use the proofreader's checklist found at the end of this essay to find those errors and then correct them.

Steroids in the Sports World

Drugs has become a major problem in sports. one of the most misabused drugs in the world of sports is steroids. Athletes turn to steroids for many reasons, but mostly because they don't want to let down their team and coach because steroids have just recently become a problem, the head committees of sports is not sure how to solve this problem. It is the thesis of this paper that all athletes should be tested for the use of steroids before a major athletic competition.

A big part of all sport competitions is the fairness issue. When using steroids they gain an advantage over their competitors because they become physically stronger. The American college of sports Medicine doesn't think that using steroids are fair. The college strongly sees the need for equality in competition and the good health of the participants. They see nonsteroid use in the best interest of all sports. Dtr. Good a clinical psychologist who specializes in chemical dependency also believe that fairness plays a big part in sports and that taking short-cuts is not fair, especially when the athlete know the rules. The governing bodies set the rules and principals regarding the use of drugs and expect them to be followed,

Proofreader's Checklist

General questions

1. Is the thesis clearly stated in the introduction?	Yes	No
2. Will the reader understand what is said?	Yes	No
3. Does the conclusion sum up the whole paper?	Yes	No
4. Is the information presented in logical order?	Yes	No
5. Does the vocabulary sound natural?	Yes	No

Paragraphs

1. Does each paragraph have a topic sentence?	Yes	No
2. Does each paragraph have at least three sentences?	Yes	No
3. Do the paragraphs flow together smoothly?	Yes	No

Sentences

1. Does every sentence express a complete thought?	Yes	No
2. Are there any run-on sentences?	Yes	No
3. Do all sentences begin with a capital letter?	Yes	No
4. Are all sentences correctly punctuated?	Yes	No
5. Do all subjects and verbs agree in person and number?	Yes	No

Words

1. Are all words spelled correctly?	Yes	No
2. Are all pronoun antecedents clear?	Yes	No
3. Are there any dangling or misplaced modifiers?	Yes	No
4. Have the best words been selected?	Yes	No

Learning to Spell Better

Spelling words in the English language is difficult because so many frequently used words do not follow any of the rules. Check your own spelling right now. Circle the word in each row that is spelled correctly.

Column A	Column B
1. acadamy	academy
2. acomodate	accommodate
3. admissable	admissible
4. accurate	acurate
5. allegiance	allegience
6. aquit	acquit
7. beleive	believe
8. bookkeeper	bookeeper
9. calender	calendar
10. confered	conferred
11. conference	conferrence
12. cushon	cushion
13. definately	definitely
14. deterant	deterrent
15. divisable	divisible
16. eficient	efficient
17. ieght	eight
18. hopeing	hoping
19. kahki	khaki
20. mischief	mischef

Answers: 1. B, 2. B, 3. B, 4. A, 5. A, 6. B, 7. B, 8. A, 9. B, 10. B, 11. A, 12. B, 13. B, 14. B, 15. B, 16. B, 17. B, 18. B, 19. B, 20. A

Spelling as seeing words

Did you know that people learn how to spell words by seeing them? Make sure you actually see words as well as hear them. Close your eyes and picture a word as you say the word aloud to yourself. Some words look alike and even sound alike, which can be confusing. Match the word in Column I to its look-alike word in Column II.

	Column I	Column II
_____	1. extant	a. duel
_____	2. dual	b. whole
_____	3. flair	c. hopping
_____	4. hole	d. hare
_____	5. hoping	e. lone
_____	6. idle	f. male
_____	7. hair	g. knew
_____	8. loan	h. extent
_____	9. mail	i. lien
_____	10. new	j. aural
_____	11. lean	k. flare
_____	12. oral	l. idol

Answers: 1. h, 2. a, 3. k, 4. b, 5. c, 6. 1, 7. d, 8. e, 9. f, 10. g, 11. i, 12. j

The problem of mispronouncing words

Do you ever mispronounce a word? The following words are often mispronounced, causing the speller to add an extra vowel. Take out the extra vowel in each word and write the word correctly.

Word	Extra vowel	Correct spelling
1. disasterous	_____	_____
2. enterance	_____	_____
3. grievious	_____	_____
4. hinderance	_____	_____

5. hundered   _____   _____

6. laundary   _____   _____

7. monsterous   _____   _____

8. partener   _____   _____

9. similiar   _____   _____

10. umberella   _____   _____

Answers: 1. disastrous, 2. entrance, 3. grievous, 4. hindrance, 5. hundred, 6. laundry, 7. monstrous, 8. partner, 9. similar, 10. umbrella

Common spelling rules

Spelling rules can be quite complex, and many have a great number of exceptions. Nevertheless, they can help you see spelling patterns.

The q rule. This is the most reliable spelling rule. The letter *q* is followed by a *u* in English words:

queen   Iraq

The ei-ie rule. Write i before *e*, except after c or when pronounced like a as in neighbor and weigh. There are some exceptions to this rule such as *protein* and *weird*.

See if you really know how this rule works. Try spelling the following words correctly by using *ei* or *ie:*

1. __ght	6. f__ld
2. y__ld	7. c__ling
3. ach__ve	8. dec__ve
4. cash__r	9. v__l
5. r__gn	10. rec__pt

Answers: 1. eight, 2. yield, 3. achieve, 4. cashier, 5. reign, 6. field, 7. ceiling, 8. deceive, 9. veil, 10. receipt

The final y rule. Words ending in y preceded by a consonant usually change *y* to *i* before any suffix except one beginning with *i*. Words ending in *y* preceded by a vowel do not change y to i before suffixes or other endings. Be careful when using this rule because there are many exceptions to it. Following the final *y* rule, add the suffixes *-ed* and *-ing* to these words:

Add *-ed*	Add *-ing*
try: _____	try: _____
stay: _____	stay: _____

Answers: tried, trying, stayed, staying

The final e rule. If the final *e* in a word is silent, it is usually dropped before a suffix beginning with a vowel but is retained before a suffix beginning with a consonant. See how well you can handle the final *e* rule as you add endings to the following words. Rewrite each word.

Add *-ing*	Add *-less*
argue: _____	care: _____
believe: _____	use: _____
judge: _____	hope: _____
like: _____	age: _____

Answers: arguing, believing, judging, liking, careless, useless, hopeless, ageless

The plural of nouns ending in y rule. If a noun ends in y preceded by a consonant, change the *y* to an *i* and add *-es* (example: baby, babies). Nouns ending in *y* preceded by a vowel add *-s* to form the plural (example: key, keys). Use the rules to write the plurals of the following nouns:

sky: _____	valley: _____
boy: _____	payday: _____
ally: _____	belly: _____

Answers: skies, boys, allies, valleys, paydays, bellies

How to learn to spell words

Use the following five steps when you want to learn to spell new words:

1. Say the word while looking at it.

2. Close your eyes, try to see the word, and then spell the word aloud.

3. Check to see if you spelled the word correctly.

4. Cover the word and write it.

5. Check again to see if you spelled the word correctly.

If the word is misspelled, go back to step one and repeat all the steps again. Use the five steps to learn how to spell any of the following common misspelled words that you cannot spell:

1. absence	14. haughtiness
2. accept	15. irritable
3. according	16. license
4. ache	17. narrative
5. across	18. peculiarities
6. beginning	19. personnel
7. careless	20. receipt
8. chocolate	21. seriousness
9. commission	22. specimen
10. despair	23. theories
11. divide	24. whether
12. enormous	25. zenith
13. fallacy	

Make a list of all words that you freqently misspell on school papers. Then use the five steps to learn these words.

Acquiring Computer Skills

This is the "Computer Age." You need to be computerwise to handle both your high school and college classes. In fact, many colleges now require you to have your own personal computer. Expertise can be gained through classes at your high school, information sessions at public libraries, and personal exploration of everything computers have to offer. Here are the basic skills that you need. Check off those that you have already acquired:

_____ keyboarding

_____ word processing

_____ using spread sheets

_____ using the Internet for research

_____ sending and receiving e-mail

_____ using the operating system (finding files, loading and removing programs, and adjusting computer settings)

Discover How to Ace Tests

Your school days are full of test-taking experiences. Many of these tests have very important outcomes. How well you do on a test may be the difference between getting an A and getting a C in a class. A high score on a college admissions test may lead to being admitted to the college of your dreams. And once you get to college, your success will hinge on how testwise you are. In this chapter, you will discover how to prepare for and take tests and think about why tests are given.

Why Tests Are Given

Tests are not given to make your life miserable. There are solid reasons they are given:

- Teachers need to find out what you have learned and what you still need to learn.

- Teachers need to evaluate their own teaching.

- By law, your achievement in different subjects often needs to be compared to that of other students in your state and the nation.

- Schools need to determine who needs or is eligible for special programs.

- Teachers need to place students of similar abilities in the same learning groups.

- College admissions officers want a more complete picture of your aptitude for college.

- Employers want to know more about your skills before they hire you.

The Key Steps to Preparing for Tests

Do you ever feel like you are hitting your head against a brick wall? Do you spend hours studying for a test, feel confident you are really prepared, and then end up not doing well on the test? Being testwise is a skill that some students master much faster than others. If you haven't mastered it yet, start now. You don't want to continue hitting your head against the test wall in college.

Ask yourself the following questions to determine if you prepare correctly for tests:

1. Do I use my class time to begin learning the material?   Yes   No

2. Do I keep up with the class reading assignments and homework?   Yes   No

3. Do I use SQ3R, outline, or take notes when I read my textbooks?   Yes   No

4. Do I take notes in class?   Yes   No

5. Do I follow a study schedule?   Yes   No

6. Do I schedule frequent review sessions for each class?   Yes   No

7. Do I make sure I know what topics will be covered on tests by listening for hints from the teacher before the test?   Yes   No

8. Do I see if there are study copies of old tests to use in preparing for tests?   Yes   No

9. Do I study what I don't know?   Yes   No

10. Do I make it a point to learn all key words in a chapter for a test?   Yes   No

11. Do I read all chapter summaries and answer all end-of-the-chapter questions in preparation for a test?   Yes   No

12. Do I schedule sufficient study time for tests?   Yes   No

Select two of the questions that you answered "No" and set yourself the goal of turning the answers to "Yes" to begin improving your preparation for tests.

Today's date: _____

Test preparation goal 1: _____

_____

_____

_____

_____

Date in four weeks: _____

Improvement noted: _____

_____

_____

_____

_____

Today's date: _____

Test preparation goal 2: _____

_____

_____

_____

_____

Date in four weeks: _____

Improvement noted: _____

_____

_____

_____

_____

Knowing what a test will be like

Half of the secret to preparing for tests is knowing what a test will be like. If the teacher does not provide you with this information, you must ask the following questions. Copy these questions into your assignment notebook so that you will be prepared with your questions before the next test.

1. What will the test cover (class discussions, chapters or pages in textbook, other)?

2. What type of test will it be (objective or essay)?

3. What kinds of questions will there be (multiple choice, short answer, true-false, other)?

4. How much time will be allotted for the test (entire class period or minutes)?

5. How will the test be answered (in blue book, on test copy, on answer sheet)?

6. Are there penalties for guessing?

7. Does every question on the test have equal value?

8. How will the test be graded?

9. What special supplies will I need?

Knowing how to study for tests

The major mistake that most students make in studying for tests is trying to reread all the material. Instead, concentrate on learning what teachers have told you will be on tests. Underline those points in your class notes, book notes, outlines, SQ3R questions, study guides, and assignments. Then review only this underlined material, paying attention to what you don't know rather than spending time on what you already know. For all classes, it is almost always essential to know the words that are listed under headings like *vocabulary, important terms,* and *word lists.* Finally, how you need to study for a test depends on what kind of test you will be taking.

Different Kinds of Tests

If you have been observant during your school years, you have noticed that sometimes your teachers give you tests that they have made, and other times they use tests made by textbook companies. Teacher-made tests usually test what teachers believe their students should have learned from both class discussion and the textbook. Textbook companies do not know what has been emphasized in class, so their tests are based on material in the textbook.

Most high school tests, no matter who made them, have an objective format, which means you are required to select or supply an answer. Less common are essay tests on which you may have to write a paragraph or even several pages on a topic. In this section, you will read about five different kinds of tests. Use a pencil or a highlighter to underline the important points that will help you improve your scores on these tests.

Multiple choice: a choice of answers

Multiple choice questions are made up of two parts. The incomplete statement or question is called the *stem*. It is followed by a list of possible answers called the *options*. The directions usually ask you to select the answer that is the best option. Problems occur when you hurry through the stem to get to the options. If you don't really understand what the stem is asking, reread it before looking at the options. Then read all the options before you select one. Remember, you are looking for the best answer—not just a good answer. Be careful because several of the options will seem good. It is helpful to cross out options that are not good answers so you can concentrate on selecting the best answer from the remaining options. Every time you eliminate even one option you increase your chances of finding the right answer. It will also help if you remember these right-answer clues:

- Options that are very precisely stated are probably correct.

- Options that are noticeably longer than others often have added information to make them correct.

- Options that seem to complete a statement but are *not* correct grammatically are incorrect.

Studying for multiple choice tests. Complete the following multiple choice test question:

Multiple choice tests require a knowledge of _____

a. details   c. principles

b. relationships   d. all of the above

Answer: (d) all of the above

Matching tests: measuring factual knowledge

Matching tests usually have two columns of information. You have the job of matching each entry in one column to the correct response in the other column. Don't be surprised if occasionally you take a matching test that has more than two columns.

Read the directions for matching tests very carefully, as answer choices can sometimes be used more than once. It is usually easier and faster if you work from the column that has the most information and try to find the correct response in the column with less information. Make sure you cross out responses as you use them unless a response can be used more than once. When you can't match an item, go on and come back to it when you have completed the column. It will be easier to determine the correct answer from the few remaining choices.

When studying for matching tests, remember that these tests are designed to measure your recall of factual information. Make sure you review specific facts, rules, formulas, dates, definitions, and names. Making and using flashcards for all the important facts is a good way to prepare for this type of test.

Complete this sample matching exercise by matching the test to what it measures:

Test	What it measures
_____ 1. achievement	a. aptitude for college work
_____ 2. college admissions	b. physical aptitudes
_____ 3. intelligence	c. knowledge in a skill area
	d. intellectual ability

Answers: 1. c, 2. a, 3. d

True-false: two choices

True-false tests give you a choice between two answers. Preparation for these tests should be similar to that for multiple choice tests as both test your knowledge of facts.

After reading a statement, decide if it is true or false. If you are unsure of the answer, remember your first response is often the correct one. You need to notice words like *usually, generally, sometimes,* and *often.* They are so broad that they are usually found in true statements. However, words like *always, all, never,* and *none* usually indicate false statements. Always answer all true-false questions, as you have a 50 percent chance of being correct.

Take the following true-false test. Circle either the T or F:

1. All tests can be prepared for in the same way. T F

2. Teachers sometimes use tests prepared by textbook companies.   T   F

3. It is never a good idea to question your teachers about what will be on a test.   T   F

4. You need to know what kind of a test you will be taking to know how to prepare for it.   T   F

Answers: 1. F, 2. T, 3. F, 4. T

Completion tests: blanks to fill in

In this type of test you are required to supply the correct word, phrase, name, number, date, or symbol to complete a statement. You will sometimes be given a word bank with the correct answers to help you out. Prepare for this test in the same way as you would prepare for any test of specific factual knowledge, but pay particular attention to vocabulary.

Use the word bank to fill in the answers on the following completion test. (You will find the words of this word bank in many essay test directions.)

word bank: analyze   discuss

explain   identify

1. Breaking something down into smaller parts to look at it closer is to_____.

2. To point out the personal distinguishing characteristics is to _____ something.

3. To consider and argue the pros and cons of something is to _____.

4. To make clear what something means is to

_____ it.

Answers: 1. analyze, 2. identify, 3. discuss, 4. explain

Essay tests: organization required

This type of test often scares students. It shouldn't, because you can figure out in advance what is going to be on an essay test. Essay questions usually cover the main points that have been discussed in your class or textbook. You will also have to know the details that are related to these main points. Unlike most of the other tests mentioned in this section, an essay test requires you to recall the answer rather than to recognize it. Prepare for this type of test by writing out answers to questions that you have made up or questions at the end of a chapter. You will frequently find that you have already answered the essay questions on a test by preparing in this way.

On essay tests, you will do better if you take a moment to organize your answers. Some students jot down a quick outline before they start writing longer essays. Strive to write clearly and to use good grammar. Make an effort to use the proper technical vocabulary, as it will let your teachers see that you not only have learned the terms but also are able to use them correctly. Remember, if you don't write something, you will not receive any credit for an answer. When you aren't sure of an answer, write down what you do know on the topic to get partial credit. Many times just starting to write an answer brings the answer to you. Don't forget to write your essays neatly so that teachers are able to read your work.

Answering an Essay Question

Try your hand at answering the following essay question: Discuss the differences between preparing for an essay test and an objective test like a multiple choice, matching, true-false, or completion test.

_____

_____

_____

_____

_____

_____

_____

_____

_____

_____

_____

Becoming an Expert at Taking Tests

Now check if you do all the right things when you take tests. Ask yourself the following questions:

1. Do I arrive at the classroom early?	Yes	No
2. Do I remember to bring all necessary supplies?	Yes	No
3. Do I remain calm?	Yes	No
4. Do I look over the entire test before beginning it?	Yes	No
5. Do I read the directions carefully before doing each section of a test?	Yes	No
6. Do I budget my time?	Yes	No
7. Do I answer the questions I know first?	Yes	No
8. Do I check my answers if there is time?	Yes	No
9. Do I believe in my ability to do well?	Yes	No

Select two questions that you answered "No" and set goals so that you will see improvement in those areas.

Today's date: _____

Test-taking goal 1: _____

_____

_____

_____

Date in four weeks: _____

Improvement noted: _____

_____

_____

_____

Today's date: _____

Test-taking goal 2:_____

_____

_____

_____

Date in four weeks: _____

Improvement noted: _____

_____

_____

_____

After the test is over

Whether you receive an A or a C, there are still things to do when a corrected test is returned to you:

- Take the time to review it.

- Find out the answers to all missed questions and write them down.

- Note what kind of errors you made so you can avoid them on future tests.

- Keep the test, if possible, so you can use it to review for semester exams.

Enhance Your School Record with Activities

Colleges seek students who have strong academic records. At the same time, they want students who have records of accomplishment outside the classroom. They are looking for the good student who played on the tennis team for four years, was active in theatrical productions, or worked at a food kitchen for the homeless. Succeeding academically while participating in outside activities demonstrates to colleges that you are an energetic person who has more than book sense.

While it is true that grades and test scores are the most important factors in admissions decisions at most colleges, a solid record of accomplishment outside the classroom through extracurricular, work, travel, and volunteer activities can tip the scales in favor of your admission, especially at selective schools. In this chapter, you will find out how you can get far more from high school than book learning by playing an enthusiastic role in activities outside the classroom.

Extracurricular Activities Are Important

Extracurricular activities are a training ground for college and career. You learn how to interact with other people as you build floats for homecoming parades, run with the cross country team every morning before school, and play in the pep band. You pick up real organizational skills by planning club meetings and the Junior Prom or by managing a sport team. What's more, you learn how to meet deadlines. Yearbooks and newspapers have to be put out on time, and minutes have to be ready for club meetings. There is also the opportunity to develop your leadership skills. You don't have to be the president of an organization to do this. You can take charge of a committee to clean up after an event or to make posters for a car wash. The more practice you have at doing these things, the more skilled you will become. There is one added dividend that you gain by participating in extracurricular activities—they are fun.

Finding your activity

You find out about what activities your school has by reading the student handbook and listening to daily announcements over the P.A. that tell you what is going on. Some schools even have open houses at the start of the school year where you can talk with representatives from each activity. With such a large choice of activities, how do you choose the ones in which you will participate? The answer is to use your interests as a guide. Check the activities on the following list that tie in most closely with your interests. Add to the list, if appropriate.

_____ sports	_____ academic clubs
_____ student government	_____ service clubs
_____ publications	_____ hobby clubs
_____ band, orchestra	_____ TV and radio stations
_____ choir	_____ drama
_____ dance	_____ speech
_____ cheerleading	_____ debate
_____ _____	_____ _____

Making a commitment

Your first year in high school is the time to investigate different types of activities to see which ones really interest you. Then in the remaining years of high school you should try to concentrate on just a few activities rather than jumping from activity to activity. The student who joins the drama club as a prompter and then earns minor roles in several plays before actually directing a play has shown the ability to make a commitment and stick to it. This is an admirable quality that college admissions officers and future bosses regard as important. An ability to commit oneself to an activity for a considerable period of time indicates maturity. Make the goal now to commit yourself to excellence in one activity this year.

Today's date: _____

Extracurricular activity goal: _____

_____

_____

_____

_____

Date in four weeks: _____

Improvement noted: _____

_____

_____

_____

_____

Using your time wisely

Some activities require extraordinary commitments of time. Sports teams practice every day. School plays require daily rehearsals. Putting out the yearbook requires a year of almost daily work sessions. Most students can handle only one major extracurricular activity at a time and do justice to their schoolwork. If you can answer the following questions with a definite "Yes," then you probably are handling the demands on your time from extracurricular activities well.

1. Do you complete all your homework every day?   Yes   No

2. Do you have sufficient time to prepare for tests?   Yes   No

3. Are you getting enough sleep?   Yes   No

4. Are you receiving the best grades you can?   Yes   No

5. Are you enjoying both your schoolwork and your extracurricular activities?   Yes   No

"No" answers indicate problems. You may be overcommitted to an activity or trying to participate in too many activities. Even though extracurricular activities provide tremendous amounts of satisfaction, remember that your first priority must be to do well in school.

Volunteering Belongs on Your Resume

So many people's lives are more pleasant because someone volunteered time to help them or their organization. High school students should try to use some of their energy for volunteer activities. Not only is volunteering very rewarding, but it also sets a precedent for a lifetime of aiding those who need some special help. The list of volunteer activities is long. Why don't you consider volunteering?

_____ assistant scout leader   _____ tutor

_____ election campaign worker   _____ sports coach

_____ library assistant   _____ reader for the blind

_____ recycling worker   _____ aide to a politician

_____ nursing home aide   _____ hospital aide

_____ food for the homeless volunteer   _____ mentor for underprivileged children

Jobs Are Learning Experiences

Finding a steady job and keeping that job shows a maturity that college admissions officers like to see in candidates for admission to their schools. They also like to see students exercise initiative in their jobs that results in promotions or interesting job assignments. Students who participate seriously in extracurricular activities may not have the time to hold part-time jobs during the school year, but they can work in the summer. Jobs offer a preview of the world of work. They teach students to arrive on time, work every day, get along with bosses who may be difficult, and stick with a task.

There are negatives to students holding jobs during the school year. Jobs can take time away from studying and encourage students to value working more than studying because working results in earning money. Jobs can also prevent students from participating in extracurricular activities.

Internships Teach About Careers

Internships offer supervised, practical work experience with companies and federal, state, and local government units. They may be paid or unpaid positions. Traditionally, internships are designed for college students; however, many are now available for high school students. Internships are an excellent way to investigate careers while gaining work experience in formal settings.

Traveling Adds to Your Experiences

Whenever you have the opportunity to travel, do so whether it is on a family trip or as an exchange student. It is an easy way to learn geography, some history, and about people in different parts of this country and the world. Being an exchange student is a particularly valuable experience as it offers an opportunity to learn about how people in other cultures live and may give you practice in speaking another language.

Activities Increase What You Learn

If you watch more than an hour of television a day, talk on the telephone for endless hours, or just hang around with your friends most of the time, you are not using your time outside the classroom to your greatest advantage. You should be spending more time on extracurricular activities, working, and volunteering. These activities add something extra to your life. They teach you skills that can't be learned in the classroom.

HOW TO GET INTO COLLEGE

Section II

The more you know about the college admissions process, the more likely you will be admitted to the college that is right for you.

Take Control of the College Admissions Process

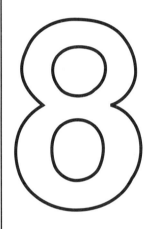

Decisions! Decisions! Decisions! There are more than 3,000 colleges in the United States. Where should you apply? Where are you likely to be accepted? Which college is right for you? How do you prepare for college admissions tests? How will you finance the cost of college? When should you start planning for college? What tasks do you need to do each year?

Planning for college is more complicated than ever before. No longer is it possible to delay organizing the college admissions process until your senior year in high school. Ideally, preparing for admission to college should begin as early as seventh and eighth grade when you begin to take challenging courses. You also need time to learn more about the person you are so that you can find the college that meets your needs and nourishes your dreams and talents.

If you don't take control of the college admissions process, you may find that you have severely limited your options in furthering your education. You may take the appropriate courses, earn the required grades, or receive satisfactory scores on admissions tests in order to be admitted to most colleges. Because there are so many tasks that need to be done at specific times, handling the college admissions process can be intimidating. In this chapter, you will learn the essential steps that will lead to your being admitted to the college that is right for you.

Keeping a Record of Your High School Career

The very first step in taking charge of the college admissions process is to start keeping a record of what you have done during high school. You will use this information when you begin to fill out college applications. Save samples of outstanding essays, art projects, and other work for possible submission with your college applications. Also keep newspaper clippings that mention your accomplishments. It is smart to keep all official reports of grades in case the school makes an error on your transcript. Also keep official results of college admissions tests. The best place to keep all these records is in a folder or large envelope. Put each year's record in a separate folder or envelope. Then store everything in one place so it will be easy to locate. A filing cabinet or an expandable pocket portfolio is a good choice.

Important information to record

You need a written record of what you have done in high school. When you are filling out college applications, it is easy to forget that you were a volunteer scout leader during the summer of your freshman year when you were also working at a fast food restaurant or that you won first place in an essay contest sponsored by a local service club when you were a sophomore. Remembering information like this could play a part in your being accepted at a college. You should keep the following information:

Grades. On many college applications, especially those for state schools, you will be asked to report what courses you have taken and the grades you have received. You will need to write down the specific name of each course. Colleges don't want to know that you studied English as a freshman in high school but, more specifically, that it was a class in composition, American literature, or speech. Be sure to indicate if a course is an honors or AP course.

Advanced Placement (AP) examinations. Colleges want to know the scores that you earned on AP exams. You may be able to earn credit and/or advanced placement based on your exam results.

Test scores. Part of the admissions process for most colleges is the taking of the SAT I, or ACT tests. Many colleges require SAT II tests. Some schools even want to know your PSAT scores. Record your test scores for easy reference.

Honors, awards, and prizes. Colleges want to see how you have been recognized in your school and community. List your academic honors as well as the awards you have received for being an outstanding artist or violinist and prizes for winning speech or 4-H contests.

Extracurricular activities. Colleges aren't just interested in your grades—they also want to know what you have done in the arts and athletics. They also want to know about your community and public service activities. Be specific in this section. List your best times if you are a swimmer or a runner. If you played first chair in the violin section of your school orchestra, say so. Tell what your responsibilities were if you were a hospital volunteer.

Employment. Schools like to know about the jobs you have held and how much time you have spent working. Not only does such information tell about your work experience, but it also explains why you may not have participated in extracurricular activities.

Travel experiences. Note trips to Washington, D.C., other states, and foreign countries. Jot down your personal reaction to each trip for possible use on essays.

Lessons. Colleges are interested in knowing about your special skills. Include your lessons on cooking, karate, and computer programming in this section.

Books. Keep a record of all the books you read during your high school years. Some colleges will want this information.

One way to record the information

Use the next pages in this book to make a record of what you have done in high school. You can either write in this book or establish a computer file to record this information.

Record of Subjects, Grades, and Scores

Keep track of your grades here. At the end of each semester, write down the exact course title for each subject and your semester grade. Include all summer school courses in this record.

Ninth grade			Tenth grade		
Course title	Fall semester grade	Spring semester grade	Course title	Fall semester grade	Spring semester grade
1. _____			1. _____		
2. _____			2. _____		
3. _____			3. _____		
4. _____			4. _____		
5. _____			5. _____		
6. _____			6. _____		
7. _____			7. _____		
8. _____			8. _____		
9. _____			9. _____		
10. _____			10. _____		
		Summer school grade			Summer school grade
_____			_____		

AP exam scores			
Ninth grade		Tenth grade	
Subject title	AP score	Subject title	AP score
1. _____		1. _____	
2. _____		2. _____	
3. _____		3. _____	

Eleventh grade				Twelfth grade		
Course title	Fall semester grade	Spring semester grade		Course title	Fall semester grade	Spring semester grade
1. _____				1. _____		
2. _____				2. _____		
3. _____				3. _____		
4. _____				4. _____		
5. _____				5. _____		
6. _____				6. _____		
7. _____				7. _____		
8. _____				8. _____		
9. _____				9. _____		
10. _____				10. _____		
		Summer school grade				Summer school grade
_____				_____		
_____				_____		

AP exam scores

Eleventh grade		Twelfth grade	
Subject title	AP score	Subject title	AP score
1. _____		1. _____	
2. _____		2. _____	
3. _____		3. _____	
4. _____		4. _____	
5. _____		5. _____	

Record of College Entrance Test Scores

PSAT

Test date: _____ Verbal score: _____ Math score: _____ Writing score: _____

Test date: _____ Verbal score: _____ Math score: _____ Writing score: _____

SAT I

Test date: _____ Verbal score: _____ Math score: _____

Test date: _____ Verbal score: _____ Math score: _____

SAT II: Subject Tests

Subject	Test date	Score
_____	_____	_____
_____	_____	_____
_____	_____	_____
_____	_____	_____
_____	_____	_____
_____	_____	_____

PLAN

Test date: _____

English score	Math score	Reading score	Science score	Composite score

ACT

Test date: _____

English score	Math score	Reading score	Science score	Composite score

Test date: _____

English score	Math score	Reading score	Science score	Composite score

Record of Honors, Awards, Prizes, and Activities

Use this page and the next two pages to keep a list of the honors, awards, and prizes you have received and the activities in which you have been involved during high school.

Honors, awards, and prizes	Grade level				Description
	9	10	11	12	

Extracurricular activities	Grade level				Approximate time spent		Positions held
	9	10	11	12	Hours per week	Weeks per year	

Sports	Grade level				Positions held, letters won, records, times, special distinctions
	9	10	11	12	

Specific nature of employment	Employer	Approximate dates of employment		Approximate number of hours per week
		from	to	

Geographic locations visited	Approximate dates	Personal reactions

Lesson areas	Approximate dates	Skill level

Books read			
Ninth grade		Tenth grade	
Eleventh grade		Twelfth grade	

Creating a Personal Calendar for the Admissions Process

Think college early. Preparation for college needs to begin in seventh grade and continue on through high school. Each year you will have different tasks that you must do in between writing papers, completing projects, studying for tests, doing your homework, participating in extracurricular activities, and working. You won't have too much to do during seventh, eighth, ninth, and tenth grades; however, you will be setting the academic standards that will be so important in college. In eleventh and twelfth grades, the admissions process intensifies and there will be things that you will need to do almost every month.

The college planning calendar that follows will help you organize your time so that the admissions process will run smoothly for you. The calendar lists the steps you should be taking every year. Read through the calendar for an entire school year at the start of the year to get an overview of what you will need to do. Then during the year check off each step as you complete it. If a step does not apply to you, (not all students need to take the SAT II, apply for financial aid, or visit colleges) check it off anyway.

By following the college planning calendar, you will avoid leaving out any vital steps in the admissions process. Although you can complete all of the steps on the planning calendar on your own, you will find it easier to complete some of these steps with the help of your guidance counselor, parents, and friends. Discuss the steps with them. Their experience can help you.

Seventh grade

Now is the time to make sure that you have the solid study skills needed for high school and college. The strength of these skills will play a major role in your future schooling. Too many students do poorly in high school and college because they don't really know how to study.

August–June

_____ Learn to be organized. Keep your school papers organized. Establish a system for recording assignments.

_____ Learn to set small realistic goals. Say, "I'm going to memorize the Gettysburg Address," not, "I'm going to do better in social studies."

Summer

_____ Read for at least thirty minutes each day.

_____ Devote time to acquiring skills or becoming more skilled in an area such as sports, art, music, and computers.

Eighth grade

Your college education will build on the skills and knowledge you acquire in earlier years. Take challenging courses and work hard to construct the solid foundation that you will need.

August–June

_____ Enroll in Algebra I or other challenging math courses so you can take chemistry, physics, trigonometry, and AP courses in high school.

_____ Learn how to study for tests by starting early and reviewing the material that you have studied.

Summer

_____ Read for at least thirty minutes each day.

_____ Continue to build your skills in such activities as sports, art, music, and computers.

Ninth grade

In four years you will be in college. This is the year to start thinking about your future. Investigate several possible careers. Find out what education each requires. This is also the year to establish a reading program that will help you improve your vocabulary.

August–September

_____ Check with your counselor to make sure that your course selections meet the requirements for high school graduation and for the colleges you may wish to attend.

_____ Set up a permanent file for your school records.

_____ Make a study schedule for yourself.

September–December

_____ Encourage your parents to attend back-to-school night so they can become familiar with your class schedule, teachers, and school.

_____ Explore extracurricular activities and begin participating in one or more activities.

_____ Begin investigating possible careers.

_____ Set up a reading program to develop your vocabulary.

January

_____ Prepare for semester tests because colleges are interested in your grades.

_____ Make any necessary program changes for the second semester.

January–May

_____ Discuss educational goals with your guidance counselor.

_____ Review your four-year plan of classes and select appropriate courses for the next school year.

_____ Prepare for second-semester tests.

June

_____ Complete your written record of ninth grade.

_____ Save samples of your work, newspaper clippings, and copies of your grades and place them in the permanent file you are keeping for ninth grade.

Summer

_____ Continue your reading program. Try to read a wide variety of materials (novels, magazines, newspapers).

_____ Obtain a PSAT or PLAN preparation book and begin to review for the test.

_____ Expand your horizons through work, sports, academic and skills programs, and volunteer activities.

Tenth grade

During this year, you need to start thinking more seriously about college. It is time to discuss financing your college education with your family and to select a few colleges of interest to you. It is also the time to begin concentrating on just a few activities so that you can make an important contribution in those activities. If you are just beginning to use this calendar, make sure that you have completed all of the necessary earlier steps so you won't miss any important parts of the admissions process.

August–September

_____ Check with your counselor that your course selections meet the requirements for high school graduation and for the colleges you may wish to attend.

_____ Discuss with your guidance counselor the advisability of taking PLAN and/or the PSAT this year.

_____ Register for the test.

September–December

_____ Take PLAN and/or the PSAT if advised to do so.

_____ Visit the guidance office to find out about college representatives visiting your school, college entrance tests, and career information.

_____ Encourage your parents to attend back-to-school night so they become familiar with your class schedule, teachers, and school.

_____ Begin to concentrate on a few extracurricular activities.

_____ Find out about NCAA requirements if you plan to play a sport in college.

_____ Begin to consider possible careers.

_____ Update your reading program and continue following it to develop your vocabulary.

January

_____ Prepare for semester tests.

_____ Make any necessary program changes for the second semester.

January–May

_____ Become better acquainted with your guidance counselor.

_____ Review your college and career goals.

_____ Select for the next school year courses that are compatible with your goals.

_____ Register and take the SAT II and AP exams for courses you are completing.

_____ Prepare for second-semester tests.

June

_____ Complete your written record of tenth grade.

_____ Save samples of your work, newspaper clippings, and copies of your grades and place them in the permanent file you are keeping for tenth grade.

Summer

_____ Continue your reading program.

_____ Visit colleges and take tours.

_____ Work, volunteer, or participate in one or more athletic, study, or skill-building programs.

Eleventh grade

This is a very important and busy year in the college admissions process. You will be taking college entrance tests, narrowing your list of possible colleges, and talking to college representatives. You should also be assuming the role of leader in your extracurricular activities.

If you are just beginning to use this calendar, make sure that you have completed all of the previous steps so you won't miss any important parts of the admissions process. Blank spaces are provided for you to enter important dates such as registration deadlines for tests, test dates, and dates of visits of college representatives to your school.

August–September

_____ Check with your counselor that your course selections meet the requirements for high school graduation and for the colleges you may wish to attend.

_____ Study college catalogs and guidebooks and visit college Web sites.

_____ Decide when you will take the necessary entrance tests for college. Enter the registration deadlines and test dates on this calendar.

_____ Check with your guidance counselor about taking the PSAT and register for the test.

_____ Attend college representative meetings to learn more about the colleges you are considering.

_____ Find out what information your school has about colleges.

_____ Investigate NCAA requirements if you plan to play a sport in college.

_____ Obtain a social security number as you will need it for college and financial aid applications.

_____ Participate fully in one or more extracurricular activities.

_____ Update and make plans to follow your reading program.

_____ _____

_____ _____

October

_____ Take the PSAT.

_____ Encourage your parents to attend back-to-school night so they become familiar with your class schedule, teachers, and school.

_____ Continue attending college representative meetings.

_____ Begin writing to colleges or visiting their on-line sites for information.

_____ Organize a filing system to store your information on individual colleges.

_____ Start thinking about teachers for possible references.

_____ _____

_____ _____

November

_____ Continue seeking information about individual colleges.

_____ Continue attending college representative meetings.

_____ Continue investigating career choices and begin to make tentative choices about careers.

_____ Make plans to visit several colleges.

_____ Discuss financing your college education with your parents. Determine the cost of attending the colleges of greatest interest to you. Estimate your Expected Family Contribution.

_____ _____

_____ _____

December

_____ Discuss your PSAT scores with your guidance counselor and use the scores to guide your college plans.

_____ Visit colleges you are interested in during your vacation.

_____ Study SAT I, SAT II, and ACT test booklets and decide which test or tests you will take.

_____ _____

_____ _____

January

_____ Prepare for semester tests because colleges are interested in your grades.

_____ Make any necessary program changes for the second semester.

_____ _____

_____ _____

January–May

_____ Review your four-year plan of classes. Pay close attention to courses that are required for college entrance.

_____ Select courses for the next school year that are compatible with your college and career goals.

_____ Reduce the number of colleges that interest you.

_____ Visit colleges for admissions interviews and tours.

_____ Talk to your guidance counselor about applying to colleges.

_____ Prepare individually or take a course to prepare for college admissions tests.

_____ Arrange to take the ACT and/or SAT I on appropriate dates.

_____ Take the SAT II and AP exams for courses you are completing.

_____ Prepare for second-semester tests.

_____ Make summer plans to work, volunteer, or attend school.

_____ _____

_____ _____

June

_____ Take the ACT, SAT I, or SAT II tests, if appropriate.

_____ Make plans to visit colleges during the summer.

_____ Complete your written record of eleventh grade.

_____ Save samples of your work, newspaper clippings, and copies of your grades and place them in the permanent file you are keeping for eleventh grade.

Summer

_____ Continue your reading program.

_____ Prepare for the ACT or SAT I, if necessary.

_____ Write or go on-line for information and applications from colleges that interest you.

_____ Visit colleges for admissions interviews and tours.

_____ Complete application forms for colleges with early deadlines.

_____ Complete housing applications, if appropriate.

_____ Work, volunteer, attend school, or participate in activities.

_____ _____

_____ _____

Twelfth grade

This is the year you must pull everything together. You should be taking challenging courses and playing an important role in extracurricular activities at your high school. Not only will you be busy with the demands of having a successful senior year, but you will also be faced with the task of completing college applications and quite possibly taking the ACT, SAT I, SAT II tests and AP exams.

Before you look over this year's calendar, make sure that you have completed all the important steps listed on the calendars for previous years. Be sure to use the blank spaces on your senior calendar to list the various deadlines that you must meet.

August–September

_____ Check with your counselor that your course selections meet the requirements for high school graduation and for the colleges you may wish to attend.

_____ Decide on a final list of colleges to which you will apply.

_____ Obtain application forms from all the colleges where you will apply for admission if you haven't already done so.

_____ Work on college applications.

_____ Select teachers to write recommendations.

_____ Visit colleges for admissions interviews and tours.

_____ Talk to college representatives who visit your high school.

_____ Decide on test dates if you will be taking the ACT, SAT I, or SAT II tests.

_____ Take the ACT, if necessary.

_____ Make plans to prepare for any tests you will be taking or retaking.

_____ Investigate scholarship opportunities. Make sure you know the NCAA requirements regarding sports scholarships.

_____ Make sure you have written down all college application deadlines and test registration deadlines and dates.

_____ _____

_____ _____

October

_____ Complete all college applications with early deadlines.

_____ Take the SAT I, SAT II, or ACT, if necessary.

_____ Prepare for any tests you will be taking.

_____ Give forms to people who will be writing letters of recommendation for you.

_____ Work on college applications and essays.

_____ Visit colleges for admissions interviews and tours.

_____ Begin applying for scholarships.

_____ Encourage your parents to attend back-to-school nights, college nights, and financial aid nights.

_____ _____

_____ _____

November

_____ Obtain financial aid forms, if appropriate.

_____ Complete all college applications.

_____ Take the SAT I or SAT II tests, if necessary.

_____ Visit colleges for admissions interviews and tours.

_____ Continue applying for scholarships.

_____ _____

_____ _____

December

_____ Complete any college applications that were not finished earlier.

_____ Start preparing financial aid forms.

_____ Continue applying for scholarships.

_____ Visit colleges for admissions interviews and tours.

_____ Take the ACT, SAT I, or SAT II tests, if necessary.

_____ _____

_____ _____

January

_____ Prepare for semester tests.

_____ Make any necessary schedule changes for the second semester.

_____ Make final college visits and participate in admissions interviews.

_____ Take the SAT I and SAT II tests, if necessary.

_____ Send in all your college applications.

_____ Make sure all recommendations, transcripts, and test scores have been sent to each college.

_____ Send in financial aid forms.

_____ Continue applying for scholarships.

_____ _____

_____ _____

February–April

_____ Make arrangements to take the ACT in February and AP tests in May, if necessary.

_____ Evaluate choices as you receive admissions decisions from colleges.

_____ Visit colleges to help make your final decision.

May

_____ Notify colleges whether you are going to accept or reject offers of admission.

_____ Take the AP exams.

_____ Study for semester tests.

_____ Make sure a transcript of your final grades and proof of graduation is sent to the college you will be attending.

_____ _____

_____ _____

May–August

_____ Keep all material sent to you by the college that you will be attending.

_____ Thank everyone who has helped you gain admittance to college.

_____ _____

_____ _____

Eliminating the Stress of College Admissions

Your mother wants you to attend the huge state university because she was a cheerleader there while you would prefer to go to a small college that doesn't even have a football team. Your guidance counselor has just told you that you should take the SAT I again. You can't think of an essay that is so innovative that it will scream, "Admit me!" Perhaps none of this will happen to you. However, trying to get into college can be quite stressful. Very few students go through the college admissions process without feeling some stress.

It is not possible to take all of the stress out of the admissions process, but you can reduce the stress by following the steps on the college planning calendar. It spreads all the things you have to do to be admitted to college over several years. Even if you wait until you are a junior before you start thinking seriously about going to college, there is still time to do most of what you should do without feeling too much pressure. When the college admissions process is organized and you don't feel rushed, you are likely to make the best possible choice of college for yourself—a decision that will affect much of what you do in the future.

Learn Everything You Need to Know About Taking Admissions Tests

Do your admissions test scores really matter? The answer is "Yes" at most four-year colleges. Of course grades, class rank, extracurricular activities, recommendations, essays, and work experiences also matter. But at many colleges, grades and test scores are the major factors in determining whether you will be accepted.

Colleges use admissions tests because the tests let them compare students across the nation to one standard. High school grading standards can vary enormously. Receiving a B in geometry at your high school with demanding Mr. Smith may have been a far greater achievement than earning an A with easygoing Ms. Jones at another school or even another teacher at your own school. In the same way, courses with identical names can vary considerably in difficulty among schools. Colleges can't tell what your school's standards are by just looking at your grades and the courses you have taken.

Because college admissions tests can play an important role in the admissions process, many students become absolutely terror stricken when they think of taking the SAT I, ACT, or SAT II Subject Tests. They forget that they have probably taken hundreds of tests and done well on them since the day they started school. In fact, most students who are applying to four-year colleges are actually experienced test takers. All they have to do to handle these tests is to approach them in the same way that they would any important test at their high schools. This means they need to know what these tests are like and then prepare for them.

In this chapter, you will find out what the different admissions tests are like and how to prepare for them. You will also learn some techniques to use in taking these tests, what your test scores mean, and when and how many times you should take these tests.

A Quick Look at Admissions Tests

Most students applying to four-year colleges take either the SAT I or the ACT. For admission to some colleges, students are also required to take SAT II: Subject Tests. Many students take the Preliminary Scholastic Aptitude/National Merit Scholarship Qualifying Test (PSAT/NMSQT) before taking the SAT I and they take PLAN before the ACT.

There is absolutely no mystery to what all these college admissions tests are like, for you can read a booklet describing each and every test. The booklets tell you exactly what type of questions to expect and how many questions there are of each type. Furthermore, there are sample test questions and even sample tests in the booklets. You can obtain these booklets from the guidance or career office at your high school. Or you can go on-line. (See Appendix B for Web sites.) The more you know about all of these tests, the better you will do on them.

PLAN: a guidance resource

Students usually take PLAN in the fall of their sophomore year on a testing date chosen by their own high schools. While the test can be considered a practice test for the ACT as it has the same multiple choice format and covers the same high school curriculum areas, it also has nonacademic sections related to future career choices. Consider PLAN a guidance resource. It lets tenth graders assess their readiness for college and see where they may need to strengthen their academic preparation. In addition, PLAN provides you with an estimated composite score of how well you are likely to do on the ACT, which will focus your preparation for this test. PLAN also gives you valuable help in career planning and provides information on your study skills.

PSAT/NMSQT: preparation for the SAT

In addition to being almost impossible to say, the PSAT/NMSQT is a multiple choice test that gives you firsthand practice for the SAT I and SAT II: Subject Test in Writing. Many students take this test, which is only given in October, as sophomores and juniors to get as much practice as possible for the SATs. Each section (verbal, math, writing) of the PSAT has questions similar to those found on the SATs. Each section has a score range from 20 to 80. Just add a zero to your PSAT scores to convert them to SAT scores. For example, a PSAT verbal score of 43 is equivalent to a 430 verbal score on the SAT I, and a math score of 55 is equivalent to 550. Once you know your scores, which are sent to schools after Thanksgiving, you can determine how much work you will need to do to prepare for the SATs. In addition, you receive information that lets you compare yourself with other college-bound students.

Besides getting a handle on the strength of their verbal, math, and writing skills as well as a forecast of SAT scores, juniors taking the test can enter the competition for scholarships from the National Merit Scholarship Corporation. Furthermore, African Americans may qualify for the National Achievement Scholarship Program for Outstanding Negro Students. And Hispanics taking the test become eligible for the College Board's National Hispanic Scholar Awards Program.

The SAT I: the major college entrance test

The SAT I is not an intelligence test. It is primarily a multiple choice test of your verbal and mathematical abilities. The test lasts for three hours and has seven sections that can appear in any order. There are two thirty-minute sections and one fifteen-minute section for both the verbal and mathematics questions. There is also a thirty-minute equating section of either verbal or math questions that does not count toward your score. This section is used to test future SAT I questions and to determine whether the test you are taking is harder or easier than past tests.

You get a verbal score and a math score. Each score ranges from 200 to 800. In addition, you receive extra information on how well you did on each area of the test plus details on how to use this information.

The ACT assessment

The official name of the other major college admissions test is the ACT Assessment, but most people simply call it the A-C-T. Although both the ACT and the SAT I are multiple choice tests, they are definitely not identical tests and test different things. While the SAT I has verbal and math tests, the ACT consists of four tests: English, mathematics, reading, and science reasoning. It is not an aptitude test like the SAT I but has questions directly related to what you have learned in your high school classes. The test takes two hours and fifty-five minutes and has 215 questions.

The ACT and SAT I have very different scoring systems. When you get your ACT test results, you receive scores and subscores for each test as well as a composite score for the entire test. Each of the four test scores and the total composite score have a range of 1 to 36. Besides receiving test results, test takers also receive a profile of their work in high school and information for career and educational planning.

The SAT II: subject tests

SAT II tests aren't like the SAT I and the ACT. They are tests of your knowledge or skills in different subjects and your ability to apply that knowledge. Altogether there are eighteen SAT II tests which fall into five general subject areas:

- English
    writing
    literature

- languages
    French   Chinese
    German   Japanese
    Modern Hebrew   Korean

Latin   English language proficiency
Spanish

- history and social studies
    American history and social studies
    world history

- mathematics
    mathematics Level IC
    mathematics Level IIC

- sciences
    biology
    chemistry
    physics

The SAT II tests are given on six dates during the school year; however, not all tests are given on each date. All the tests take one hour of testing time, and you can take as many as three tests on any one test date. All of the tests are multiple choice except for the English writing test, which has an essay as well as multiple choice questions.

The more selective a college is, the more likely it is you will have to take SAT II tests. Some colleges request that you take one or two specific tests, usually the English writing test and a mathematics test. Others let you choose the tests that you prefer.

Each subject test has a score range of 200 to 800. Besides being considered in the admissions process, these scores are used by colleges for placement in the freshman and higher-level courses.

Never choose subject tests without looking at samples. You may find the questions in one subject area to be much easier than those in another. Be sure also to look closely at the two mathematics tests to determine which level is most appropriate for you. And you will need to decide if you should take a reading-only language test or one that also has a listening section.

Choosing between the SAT I or ACT

Most four-year colleges accept scores from either the SAT I or the ACT. Some students perform much better on one test than the other. Taking sample tests under testing conditions can give you a good idea of how you are likely to score on each test. Or you can even take both tests. Most colleges use the higher test score in considering you for admission.

Careful Timing on Admissions Tests

Without some advance planning of your testing schedule, disaster may occur. You may find that you don't have time to study for a required SAT II: Subject Test or to retake the SAT I or ACT. You may also find you have to take a test the same day as the state cross country meet or your brother's wedding. Furthermore, colleges have deadlines for when these tests must be taken.

Testwise students don't wait until their senior year to begin taking admissions tests. Students planning to take the ACT usually take PLAN as sophomores and the ACT in the spring of their junior year. Students can take the PSAT as sophomores, but most wait until they are juniors to take this test. Then in the spring of their junior year, they take the SAT I so that they have time to retake the test if necessary. Knowing what their test scores are on the ACT or SAT I at an early date helps students choose the colleges to which to apply. Testwise students also take SAT II: Subject Tests shortly after completing a course. This could mean taking the SAT II test in a subject like biology as early as May or June of the sophomore year.

Planning your test schedule

The first step in planning your test schedule is to find out which admissions tests the colleges you are seriously considering want you to take. You will find this information in college brochures and college guidebooks as well as on college Web sites.

Complete the following chart so that you have a clear picture of which college admissions tests you need to take.

Tests Required for Admission to College

Name of college	ACT or SAT I (required)	Names of SAT II: Subject Tests (if required)
		_____ _____ _____
		_____ _____ _____
		_____ _____ _____
		_____ _____ _____
		_____ _____ _____

Choosing your test dates. Each year the ACT, SAT I, and SAT II tests are given in the same months. Most students take the SAT I and ACT in the spring of their junior year. Use the information in the following chart to decide when you will take each test:

Schedule of Test Dates

Test dates	Test given
September*	ACT
October	SAT I, SAT II, ACT
November	SAT I, SAT II
December	SAT I, SAT II, ACT
January	SAT I, SAT II
February**	ACT
March/April ***	SAT I
April	ACT
May	SAT I, SAT II
June	SAT I, SAT II, ACT

*The ACT is not given in every state on this date.
**The ACT may not be given in New York on this date.
***Whether this test date is in March or April varies.

Creating your own test schedule. You need to consider the following points in planning your own test schedule:

- You cannot take the SAT I and SAT II: Subject Tests on the same day.

- You may want to take the ACT or SAT I more than once.

- You can take only three SAT II: Subject Tests in a test session.

- You must consider which SAT II: Subject Tests are given on each date.

- Colleges have certain deadlines for receiving test scores.

- It is helpful to have time to prepare for admissions tests.

In order to complete your personal test schedule, you have to look at test registration booklets to determine the actual test dates and registration deadlines. Once your schedule is complete, be sure to write all the test and registration dates on your planning calendar in Chapter 8 and on the following chart:

Student's Test Schedule

Name of test	Test date	Registration deadline

Registering for Tests

You will find all the information you need about registering for tests in the registration bulletins put out for the ACT, the SAT I, and SAT II: Subject Tests. When you fill in paper or on-line registration forms, be sure to use the same name that you are going to use on all your college applications in order to avoid confusion later on. You need to know your social security number and your high school code number which is on test posters at your school or available at the career or guidance office. Write this information down now so you can use it when registering for tests:

Last name   First name   Middle initial

_____   _____   _____

Social Security number: __ __ __-__ __-__ __ __ __

High school code: __ __ __-__ __ __

A free information service. When you are filling in the registration form for the ACT or the SAT I, you can indicate that you want certain information about yourself sent to colleges, governmental agencies, and scholarship agencies. If you do, you may be deluged with mail from colleges that are interested in having students like you.

Test questions and answers. For certain test dates you can get a copy of the test you took, your answers, and the correct answers. This is helpful information if you plan to retake a test.

Registration deadlines. If you should miss a registration deadline or decide rather suddenly to take a test, don't despair: all of the tests have late registration dates. You may even be able to take the SAT I, SAT II, or ACT tests as a standby.

Your admission ticket. You should receive an admission ticket well before each test. Be sure to contact the testing agency if you have not received your ticket before the time stated in the registration bulletin. When you receive your ticket, make sure that all of the following information is accurate: your name, sex, birth date, Social Security number, telephone number; the name of the test; the test date; and the test center. Follow instructions to correct or add information as necessary.

How to Prepare for Admissions Tests

Even if you are a straight-A student who aces every test, you will probably do better on college admissions tests if you spend some time preparing for them. The bare minimum of preparation for these tests is to read test bulletins. In fact, you should read these bulletins several times because they provide so much helpful information.

Reading a test bulletin will help you become familiar with the content and organization of a test and will provide you with test-taking tips. If you don't read a bulletin before taking a test, you simply won't know what to expect on the test. Furthermore, everything that you see on the test you will be seeing for the first time—a serious disadvantage.

Practicing with actual tests

The more familiar you are with the format of a test, the less anxious you will feel about taking it. Besides, when you are familiar with a test, you can devote all of your time to answering the questions rather than worry about understanding the directions. The best way to become familiar with a test is to practice on actual tests that have been given in years past. Both the College Board (SAT I and SAT II) and ACT publish several books of sample tests that are available in bookstores and from the test companies. Consult the SAT and ACT registration bulletins for information about obtaining sample tests.

When you work with practice tests, it is important to take a number of them under the same time limits you will have on the test day. This will teach you how to pace yourself on the test.

Preparing for the SAT I

There has been a great amount of controversy over how to prepare for the SAT I. Some people feel the answer lies in getting coaching, while others favor using vocabulary-building programs, extensive reading, doing well in your classes, or using preparation guides and computer programs. All of these strategies can be helpful. How successful any form of preparation is depends largely on your motivation to improve your vocabulary and math skills, because that is what the SAT I is all about. When students work hard in these two areas for weeks before a test, they do better on the SAT I.

The experts agree that cramming right before the test rarely results in significantly higher scores. And that, of course, is what preparation is all about—getting the highest scores you can get.

Vocabulary-building programs. The verbal part of the SAT I is based almost entirely on vocabulary. The larger your vocabulary, the better you will do. The most effective way to build your vocabulary is to read, read, and read. In Chapter 4, it was suggested that you start a reading program when you enter high school. Even if you haven't been much of a reader, extensive reading in your junior year can improve your vocabulary and comprehension skills. You can also improve your vocabulary by working with vocabulary lists that contain words frequently found on the SAT I.

Preparation books and computer programs. By working alone with SAT I preparation books and computer programs, you can become more familiar with the test format as well as increase your math and vocabulary skills. Some students like the immediate feedback offered by computer programs that let you see at once whether an answer is correct as well as the reasoning behind each answer.

Coaching courses. There is now agreement that coaching can improve test scores. The question is by how much, since this coaching can be quite expensive—into the hundreds of dollars. In general, the lower the score, the greater the improvement, provided a student works hard. These courses provide review, improve skills (especially math skills), give students practice in taking the test, and make students feel more comfortable about taking the tests.

Preparing for the ACT

The ACT covers the knowledge, understanding, and skills that you have acquired throughout your schooling; therefore, last-minute preparation for this test is not very effective. The first thing that you need to do is become acquainted with the organization of the test and the types of questions. Then you must familiarize yourself with the content of the individual tests. If there are areas that you have not studied or that are not fresh in your mind, concentrate on learning this material.

Preparing for SAT II: Subject Tests

Since you will be tested on factual knowledge on the SAT II: Subject Tests, what you have learned in school plays a large role. You will get the best idea of what you need to know for any SAT II test by studying sample tests. Then by taking sample tests, you will find out what your weaknesses are and can devote your time to reviewing these areas in your textbooks. It is possible to get an expert evaluation of your essay for the writing test by submitting it to the College Board's Online Essay Evaluation Service (http://www.collegeboard.org).

Ready, Set, Go—Test Day!

Give yourself the advantage of being organized for an admissions test. First of all, avert disaster on the morning of the test by making sure several days before where your test center is if it isn't in your own school. There are horror stories about students who couldn't find a test center until after a test had started.

Don't turn the night before the test into an all-night cram session. Limit your time to reviewing what you have been studying. Then go to bed and set your alarm so you will have time to get up and leave for the test without a frantic Dagwood Bumstead exit.

Remember that getting off to a flying start on a test doesn't mean arriving with unsharpened pencils a minute before the test is to start. Here is your checklist of things to put in one spot the night before a test:

_____ your admission ticket

_____ four sharpened (soft-lead) no. 2 pencils and a very good eraser

_____ identification that meets the requirements stated in the registration bulletin

_____ a watch, as test centers are not required to provide clocks

_____ an acceptable calculator with extra batteries for ACT, SAT I, and SAT II math subject tests

_____ an acceptable cassette player with earphones for SAT II language tests with listening

_____ a snack for your break

Test-taking strategies

Before you arrive at the test center to take an admissions test your test-taking strategy should be set. By reading the test bulletin, you have learned specific test-taking tips that the testmaker believes will help you on the test. Remember that the easy questions are usually at the beginning of a group of questions. Be aware of how tests are scored. There are penalties for wrong answers on the SAT I and SAT II, so guess smart and omit questions when you have no idea of the answer for these tests. Also, use your test booklet for scratch work. You can cross off answers you know are wrong and circle questions you have skipped. Having done practice tests, you should know what a test is like and how to pace yourself to do your best. Avoid spending too much time on one question.

There are only a few other strategies for test day to ensure that the outcome is as successful as possible:

- Arrive early enough so you can choose the best seating. You don't want to be distracted because your chair is uncomfortable or you are sitting next to a heating or air-conditioning unit. Ask to be moved if it is necessary.

- When you receive your test, make sure that both the test booklet and answer sheet are complete and legible.

- Check your answer sheet periodically to make sure that your answers are in the right place and sufficiently darkened.

- Be sure to erase any extraneous answers on the answer sheet as they can cause your test to be scored incorrectly.

After You Receive Your Scores

Don't panic if your scores on admissions tests are not as good as you had wished. On the other hand, if they are great, don't assume that you will be admitted to the college of your dreams. Your test scores are only one part of the decision of a college to admit you.

What you want to do with your test scores is evaluate whether they meet the requirements of the schools that interest you. State colleges tend to have a minimum or suggested score that students should meet, while private schools tend to be more fuzzy about what their requirements are, listing only the average scores of recent classes. You can use the following chart to evaluate your test scores and determine whether to retake a test:

Possible colleges	Suggested scores			Actual scores		
	ACT	SAT I		ACT	SAT I	
		V	M		V	M

Should you retake a test?

Some students should retake admissions tests. If your scores do not meet the requirements of a state school or are significantly below the average scores of students accepted at selective schools, you need to retake the test. Also consider retaking a test if you need a higher score for a scholarship. Students' scores usually go up the second time they take a test. There is very little reason, however, for students with exceptionally high scores to retake a test as they may not do as well the second time. You can, of course, retake admissions tests more than once. Colleges typically use the higher test score for admission eligibility.

What Else You Need to Know

You need to read test bulletins carefully to find out about the rules to follow when taking these tests. You also need to understand how the test results will be reported to you and how to have them reported to colleges. Be aware that the test scores can be cancelled immediately after or within a short time of taking admissions tests. Also, you can request a review of your SAT II: Subject Tests scores before sending them to colleges. Details on reporting, reviewing, cancelling, and rescoring tests are given in your test bulletins.

Discover How to Find the College That Is Right for You

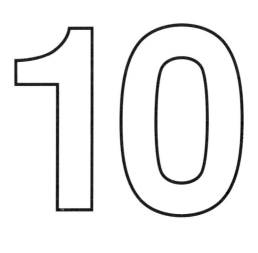

There is no one "perfect" college for you, but you can find a school that fits your needs and is right for you. This is true whether you have a straight A or a C average, are an athletic superstar or a nonparticipant in extracurricular activities, or have high or low scores on admissions tests. The hard part of this task is sifting through the great number of colleges to find the best one for you. It involves making one of the first big decisions of your life. However, a lot of people—parents, counselors, friends, and college admissions officers—will give you valuable help. And it can even be an enjoyable experience once you have determined your basic needs and preferences and applied them to schools that you are considering.

In this chapter, you will be given a framework to use in choosing the colleges that most closely meet your needs. It will not remove all of the stress from deciding where to apply, but it will give you a sequence of steps that will make the task much easier. You will pinpoint what you are looking for in a college, find out how to discover schools that meet your basic needs, and learn how to narrow your choices to the few schools to which you will apply.

Step One: Determine What You Want in a College

No two students are looking for the same qualities in a college. Your choices will not be the same as your best friend's. You need to find schools that will prepare you for careers that you are considering. Then you have to decide on what aspects of college life (school size, location, living arrangements, and so on) are most important to you.

Consider your goals

Think back now to the goals you listed as possible career choices in Chapter 1. Were they definite choices or just fuzzy ideas about your future? Either answer affects your decision about where you should apply to college. For example, if you know that you want to be an engineer, it only makes sense to apply to schools that offer degrees in engineering. And obviously students who want to devote all their time to the study of art or music should look for schools that will let them concentrate on those areas.

If you are not certain about what you would like to do in the future but think that it will be in science or the liberal arts, you need to apply to schools that offer those particular curriculums. And if you are very uncertain about your career goals, you need to find schools that offer a very wide range of courses. You should also realize that for many careers you can get all the preparation that you need at a two-year technical or community college.

Choosing an academic program. Your first consideration in narrowing the list of colleges is to find colleges that offer academic programs that will allow you to achieve your career goals. Take the time right now to check what type of academic program you need:

_____ with an emphasis on liberal arts

_____ with an emphasis on science and math

_____ with a broad curriculum including liberal arts and science

_____ professional: architecture, education, nursing, home economics, engineering, physical therapy, and other professions

_____ specialty (art, drama, mining)

_____ technical with a stress on career education

Choosing a major. The field of study in which a student specializes and receives his or her degree is called a *major*. Some students know what their majors will be when they enter college, but most do not. Furthermore, many college students choose a major only to switch to another field later on. Even Albert Einstein said that he would not choose to major in science if he had his life to live over. Nevertheless, if you feel strongly that you want to major in Japanese or architecture, make sure that you are applying to colleges that offer these majors. List the major or majors that interest you so you can consider them when applying to colleges:

Possible major or majors: _____

Your college profile

Once you have determined what type of academic program you need in a college, you are ready to figure out more precisely what you want in a college. Answering the following questions will give you a better idea of what your preferences are. Then you can investigate which colleges match your preferences most closely.

Location

1. Where would you like to go to college?

   a. the East

   b. the Midwest

    c. the South

    d. the Southwest

    e. the West

2. Where would you prefer to live while you are in college?

    a. a metropolitan area

    b. a large city

    c. the suburbs

    d. a small town

    e. a rural area

3. How far would you like to be from your home?

    a. less than one hour by car

    b. two to four hours by car

    c. in a nearby state

    d. in another region of the country

College environment

1. What type of school would you like to attend?

    a. public

    b. private

    c. with a religious affiliation

2. What type of student body would you like?

    a. single sex

    b. primarily female

    c. primarily male

    d. coeducational

3. What size student body most appeals to you?

    a. fewer than 1,500 students

    b. 1,500 to 3,000 students

    c. 3,000 to 5,000 students

    d. 5,000 to 10,000 students

    e. more than 10,000 students

4. What type of living arrangements would you prefer?

    a. on-campus dormitory

    b. sorority or fraternity

    c. off campus

    d. at home

    e. other: _____

5. What type of campus activities would you like?

    a. a wide variety of extracurricular activities

    b. a broad athletic program

    c. a lively social life

    d. a strong focus on religion

    e. other: _____

    f. some combination of the above (circle choices)

6. What type of atmosphere is right for you?

    a. with an emphasis on academics

    b. with an emphasis on social life

    c. a balance between academics and social life

Academic offerings

1. What types of programs do you want a college to offer?

    a. co-op program (work/study)

    b. overseas study

    c. internships

    d. independent studies

e. assistance for learning disabilities

f. other: _____

2. What type of classes are important to you?

a. small classes

b. large classes

c. lecture-oriented classes

d. discussion-oriented classes

e. some combination of the above (circle choices)

Facilities

What facilities at a college are important to you?

a. number of computer terminals

b. number of volumes in the library

c. student union

d. sports facilities

e. other: _____

f. some combination of the above (circle choices)

College costs

Which description best fits your financial concerns?

a. Cost is not important.

b. Cost is a minor consideration.

c. I will need some financial aid.

d. I will need major financial aid.

Admissions competitiveness

In which level of difficulty will you fit?

a. noncompetitive (almost all high school graduates are admitted)

    b. minimal requirement (most applicants are in the bottom half of their class)

    c. selective (most applicants are in the top half of their class)

    d. highly selective (more than 75 percent of applicants are in the top half of their class)

    e. extremely selective (more than 75 percent of applicants are in the top 10 percent of their class)

Additional criteria

Are there any other aspects that you would like to consider in your search for a college that is right for you? Perhaps you would like freshman seminars or easy access to your professors. List your additional college search criteria here:

1. _____

   _____

   _____

2. _____

   _____

   _____

3. _____

   _____

   _____

Step Two: Prioritize Your Selection Criteria

You should now have a good idea of the major aspects of college life that are important to you. Carefully study the choices that you have made. Then write down the six most important characteristics that you are looking for in a school. For example, you might decide on the following criteria: (1) the school should be near a beach; (2) the school should have a drama department that produces several plays each year; (3) the school should have an overseas study program; (4) the school should be large and offer a very broad curriculum; (5) the school should have fraternities; (6) the school should have a challenging curriculum.

1. _____

_____

_____

2. _____

_____

_____

3. _____

_____

_____

4. _____

_____

_____

5. _____

_____

_____

6. _____

_____

_____

Step Three: Obtain Information About Different Colleges

Before you begin to select the colleges where you will apply, you need to gather information about many different schools. This is one of the easiest parts of the admissions process. In fact, good students almost drown in the amount of material that is sent to them. You will probably start getting mail from colleges as soon as you take one of the admissions tests if you checked the box on the registration form allowing information about yourself to be sent to different colleges. Following are some other ways to get information about colleges.

College guidebooks

A good place to start looking for information is in the big college guidebooks that have facts on hundreds of schools. Appendix A has a list of these guidebooks that offer a wealth of factual information about such considerations as costs, admissions requirements, programs of study, financial aid, selectivity, student]life, environment, majors, and profiles of the freshman class.

Web sites

The new kid on the block in the admissions process is the Internet. Just about every school has a Web site filled with information about admissions, housing, financial aid, majors, courses, faculty, sports, recreation, the campus, the local community, and even the weather. You can find many schools by simply entering the URL http://www.*schoolname*.edu. For example, the URL for Indiana University Bloomington is http://www.indiana.edu. Note in Figure 10.1 the topics that you can find out about by visiting the "Student and University Life" page at Indiana University Bloomington.

College mailings

When you want more information about a particular college than you can find in a guidebook or at its Web site, write or e-mail the college and ask for it. If you want specific information about, for example, a co-op program or scholarships, you must request it. Just an e-mail message, brief letter, or a postcard like the following one is all you

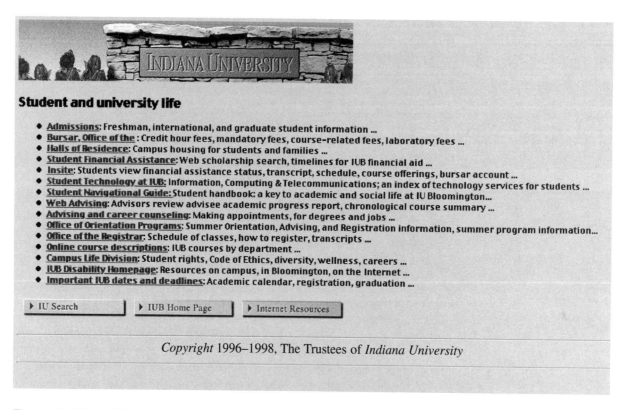

Figure 10.1 *You will find in Appendix B additional Web sites that will be helpful in the admissions process.*

need to send to a college. Don't forget to include your name and address. You can get the school's mailing and e-mail addresses from a guidebook or the college Web site.

Office of Admissions
Name of College
Address

I am currently a *(year in school)* at *(name of school)*. I am interested in receiving information about *(name of college)*. Please send me *(an application form, catalog, financial aid information and forms, or whatever specific information you want)*.

Thank you.

(Your Name)
(Your Address)
(City, State, ZIP)

Students asking for information from colleges are usually sent brochures or viewbooks. This information features pictures of the campus, faculty, and students as well as information about entrance requirements and procedures, housing, social life, the faculty, course offerings, special programs, athletic teams, and extracurricular activities. Because catalogs are expensive to produce, you may not receive one unless you request it. Once you have contacted a college and requested information, you should expect to continue receiving mail from that college.

Catalogs

College catalogs are not meant to be read from cover to cover but to be used as references for specific details about a school. Besides offering information about the school, admissions, policies, procedures, and the faculty, catalogs give descriptions of the courses and course requirements for different majors. Instead of sending for catalogs, you may be able to find them at many libraries and high school guidance or career offices as well as access this information from college Web sites.

Videos

Videos give you a sense of what a campus is like. They help you understand its lifestyle. On videos you can see students and faculty members talking about course offerings, special programs, housing, sports, and extracurricular activities. In many ways, seeing a video is the next best thing to visiting a college campus. You can find videos in school and public libraries and high school guidance or career offices. Some schools will even send you videos or offer them on-line.

Visits from college representatives

Watch for the visits of college representatives to your high school. By attending a session with a visiting representative, you can learn two very important types of information: what a school is like and what type of students it wants. In addition, you can receive expert answers to your specific questions about a college.

College information nights and college fairs

At a college information night or a college fair you have the chance to see in a short amount of time what a great number of colleges from different areas of the country offer. You can pick up college brochures, viewbooks, and catalogs and sign up for more material to be sent to you. You also have the chance to chat briefly with different college representatives.

Visits to colleges

A visit to a college lets you get the feel of a campus and helps you find out if you will be comfortable there. While you are visiting a college, you can learn even more about it through attending an information session and scheduling an interview. In the next chapter, you will learn what to see and do when you visit campuses as well as how to prepare for interviews.

An overlooked source of information—people

Students often overlook getting information about different colleges from people they know. Quite often these people can give them a good picture of what college and college life are really like. Talking to people gives you the chance to add a personal touch to the information you are gathering about colleges. Have you talked to the following people about college?

- your parents

- your brothers and sisters in college

- your high school guidance or career counselor

- teachers

- older friends in college

- friends of your parents

- people working in careers that interest you

- alumni of a specific college

Private counselors. Private counselors provide students with information about colleges and help students find colleges that match their interests and abilities. Some of these counselors also help students complete their applications. This type of counseling can be expensive. Be sure to check the background of these counselors.

Step Four: Make a Tentative List of Colleges

Once you have some information about colleges, you are ready to make a tentative list of schools to investigate further. You don't want to have too long a list—twenty is probably a maximum number—because you want to learn all about these colleges and that takes time and effort. Remember, this is not the final list of colleges to which you will actually apply but a list of colleges that interest you for a variety of reasons.

Organization of information on colleges

You need to have a system to organize all the mailings you receive from colleges and the information you pick up at college fairs, college nights, and the guidance office at your school, and from the Internet. You don't have to have a sophisticated filing system to keep track of all the materials, but you should place all the material about one school in the same envelope or folder.

As you read through the material, sort it into at least three categories. The material from schools that do not meet your basic goals should simply be thrown out. The rest of the material can be divided into two categories: schools that interest you a great deal and schools in which you have some interest.

Your tentative list

Put on your tentative list of schools all those in the "schools that interest you a great deal" category. Add the schools that you have always thought about attending. Then add the schools that your parents think are good choices for you. Don't forget to put a state college or university on your list. Finally, if you have room on your list, add schools that friends, relatives, and counselors have recommended to you. You can also add schools in which you "have some interest."

Draw the computer into your search for schools. Go to a Web site (see Appendix B) that will let you use many of your search criteria to find a school. Type in the characteristics you want, like size, location, cost, and major, and a list of colleges will appear on your screen.

Check your list. You may need to add or subtract some schools. You want to have a realistic list that offers you a number of options. You should be able to answer "Yes" to all of the following questions about your tentative list:

1. Are there schools on the list to which you will definitely be admitted? _____ (Many colleges, including some state schools, admit all high school graduates.)

2. Are there schools on the list to which you are likely to be admitted because your grades and test scores meet the minimum entrance requirements? _____

3. Are there schools on your list whose admissions requirements are a reach for your qualifications? _____ (Outstanding strengths in extracurricular activities can sometimes lead to admission to schools where your grades and test scores are below the entrance requirements.)

4. Are there schools that are affordable on your list? _____ (Most students receive some form of financial aid, which is discussed in Chapter 13.)

5. Do all the schools on your list meet your academic program and career requirements? _____

Reduce your list to twenty schools. If your tentative list is too large, reduce it by finding out more about individual schools so you can select those that are most appealing to you in such areas as course offerings, location, environment, and cost. Then write your list of tentative schools in the following chart. The list of schools that you visit and to which you apply should come from this group of colleges.

Tentative List of Schools

1. _____   8. _____   15. _____

2. _____   9. _____   16. _____

3. _____   10. _____   17. _____

4. _____   11. _____   18. _____

5. _____   12. _____   19. _____

6. _____   13. _____   20. _____

7. _____   14. _____

Step Five: Narrow Your Choices of Colleges

Once you have a list of colleges to consider, it is time to learn more about these schools. Read about the schools in guidebooks, visit their Web sites, send for materials, and try to visit them. Be sure to talk to people about the schools. Remember that the fact your Aunt Betty went to the state university and was absolutely miserable there because it was so large is no reason to assume that a large school would not work for you. While you are narrowing your list of college choices, be sure to involve your parents and school counselors in the process.

Review now the list of six priorities you chose for your selections criteria on page 180. Write those criteria in the chart on page 188. Place a check mark in the appropriate space on the chart whenever a college on your tentative list meets a specific criteria.

Selecting your best choices

Look carefully at how the different colleges in your chart compare to each other. Note which colleges most closely match your selection criteria and write them down on the chart on page 189. These are the colleges that are most right for you. If you do not have ten colleges that closely match your criteria, you may want to do more research in order to expand the list of colleges you are considering.

Comparing College Choices

Name of college	Selection criteria					
	_____	_____	_____	_____	_____	_____
1.						
2.						
3.						
4.						
5.						
6.						
7.						
8.						
9.						
10.						
11.						
12.						
13.						
14.						
15.						
16.						
17.						
18.						
19.						
20.						

List of Preferred Schools

1. _____   6. _____

2. _____   7. _____

3. _____   8. _____

4. _____   9. _____

5. _____   10. _____

Cost. You can't finalize your list of colleges until you consider the cost of attending college. Going to college can be very expensive. Some selective private schools now cost almost $30,000 a year, and state-supported schools can cost over $8,000 for just tuition and room and board. Use the financial information found in college profiles in guidebooks and at Web sites to determine roughly what the colleges on your list will cost to attend.

Even though college is expensive and becoming more expensive each year, financial aid makes it possible for most college applicants to attend college. The majority of students at almost all colleges receive some kind of financial aid. While guidebooks and Web sites give information only about typical aid packages, students can receive considerably more or less than the amounts stated. You must also realize that few financial aid packages cover the entire cost of college. Read Chapter 13 for a thorough discussion of financial aid.

You need to have frank talks with your parents or guardians about how much they will be able to contribute to your education. You may need to include more schools with lower costs on your preferred list. You also need to investigate fully all the options available for financial help. It is a good idea to include a visit to the financial aid office at every college that you tour.

Selectivity. Some schools will admit all high school graduates while others are so selective that only 13 percent of those who apply are admitted. Determine how your grades and test scores compare to those required for schools on your preferred list.

Arrange the schools on your preferred list in three groups to reflect the difficulty you will encounter in being admitted to those schools. In the first group, place those

College Costs

Name of college	Tuition	Room and board	Total*

*Total does not include books, transportation, or personal expenses.

schools that are "sure admissions" because your grades and test scores are well above the minimum required. In the second group, list the colleges that are "probable admissions" since the average grades and test scores of those admitted are similar to yours. And, finally, put in the third group those schools to which you only stand a chance of being admitted. You should have at least one school in each group.

Selectivity List

Sure admissions	Probable admissions	Uncertain admissions

Admissions Requirements

Name of college	Required GPA*	My GPA	Minimum required			My scores		
			SAT I			SAT I		
			V	M	ACT	V	M	ACT

*GPA—grade point average

Step Six: Make Your Final Choices

How many colleges should you apply to? There is no right number. For most students, the right answer is probably somewhere between three and seven schools. Students should apply to more than one school because acceptance is not always a certainty and it is good to have a choice.

Choose the final list of schools that you would most like to attend and to which you will apply. Make sure that you choose at least one school in the "sure admissions" category. It is also a good idea to reach a little, so put at least one school from the "uncertain" category on your final list. Finally, choose your favorites from the "probable" category. Then write down the names of the colleges, listing them by first to last choice.

Final College Admissions Choices

1. _____   5. _____

2. _____   6. _____

3. _____   7. _____

4. _____

Now that you have carefully selected the schools to which you will apply, try to visit as many of them as you can before you begin filling out your applications.

Make the Most of College Visits and Interviews

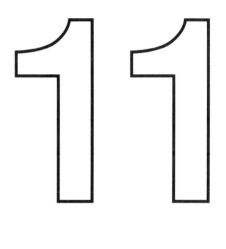

One of the many steps in the admissions process is the campus visit. It's an opportunity to get more information about the colleges you are considering. You may discover that the atmosphere of a small school your cousin Fred recommended is just perfect for you even though earlier you had your heart set on attending the state university. You may find yourself drawn to a school because of the friendliness of the students and faculty members. The campus visit is also an opportunity for interviews with admissions officers who can tell you more about the school and answer questions about the admissions process.

Visiting Colleges That Interest You

You can look at brochures, viewbooks, videos, and Web sites and read profiles of schools, but nothing is the same as walking around a campus, talking to students and faculty members, and spending a night in a dorm. By visiting a campus, you can tell what a college is like and whether it is the right one for you. Visits also let you notice the subtle differences between colleges, which is very helpful in your decision process. Of course, you won't be able to visit all of the schools on your tentative list, but you should try to visit the most appealing ones.

The time to visit colleges

Most students visit colleges in the spring of their junior year, the summer before their senior year, or the fall of their senior year. Visits to several colleges can be part of a family vacation. You can also visit colleges when they hold special preview or college days for high school students. A casual visit to a nearby campus should be made sometime during the first two years of high school. Such a visit can be very motivational, giving you a solid reason to do better academically or to shine in extracurricular activities. It is decidedly helpful to have visited a campus before applying for admission.

The best time to visit a college is during the week when school is in session. Try to avoid finals week or big game weekends so that you can get a picture of everyday campus life. While admissions officers have more time to talk to you in the summer, at that time there may be few or no students on campus.

The more time you can spend on a campus, the better you will be able to tell what the college is like. Ideally, you should spend a day and a night at a school. By spending a night, especially a weeknight, you can get a good idea of how much studying, talking, and partying the students do at night and how it fits with your lifestyle.

Preparing for a college visit

You, not your parents or guardians, should do most of the preparation for college visits. This includes contacting the admissions office for an interview, finding out the times of campus tours and group information sessions, and making arrangements to stay overnight in a dorm. Do this by phone. Most schools have toll-free numbers. If you have special interests that you want to pursue in college, you should mention this to the admissions office before you arrive on campus. The office may be able to arrange for you to visit classes, talk to faculty members, or visit with coaches and students. Preparing for a visit also includes reading about a school so you know what you want to see and what questions you want answered.

What to see and do

Colleges want to interest visiting students in applying to and enrolling in their schools. Most schools have well-organized tours that show off their best features. Many also have group information sessions at which you can learn about academic programs, housing, social life, and admissions as well as ask questions. You can get a good picture of a school in a limited amount of time by going on a tour and attending a group information session.

Begin your college visit at the admissions office where you can join tours or group information sessions or, if necessary, pick up a map for a self-guided tour. How much you can see and do during a visit naturally depends on how much time you are able to spend on the campus. To have a good campus visit you should at least take the following steps:

- Take a tour of the campus, which includes seeing classrooms, the library, the student union, and student housing.

- Attend a group information session.

- Pick up a copy of the student newspaper.

- Take pictures.

- Visit the financial aid office for applications and information if you will be applying for aid.

If you plan on spending a full day at a college, you will want to add the following activities to your list so you can become even better acquainted with a school:

- Sit in on at least one class in an area that interests you.

- Have a meal in a campus dining hall.

- Find out where students can find a snack when they are tired of dorm food.

- Talk to students about what the school is like.

- Shadow a student.

- Talk to faculty members to learn more about programs that interest you.

- Talk to coaches if you want to participate in sports on the varsity level.

- Talk to students involved in extracurricular activities that you would like to pursue on campus.

- Wander around the school just absorbing the atmosphere.

- Visit special facilities that interest you (performing arts centers, science labs, tennis courts).

Once you have visited a college, take a few minutes to jot down your reactions to the school. Be sure to include this information:

- comments on the buildings, setting, and total environment;

- opinions of the students and faculty;

- what you liked best;

- what you liked least; and

- the names and addresses of people to contact for more information.

Caution: Don't let a poor guide, miserable weather, or terrible food totally influence your impression of a school.

Having a Successful Interview

There are two excellent reasons for scheduling a college interview. First, it is an opportunity for you to become a real person to admissions officers instead of a combination of grades, scores, and activities on an application. Second, it lets you learn more about a college.

The importance of the interview in the admissions process varies enormously. It is certainly not the most important factor in being admitted to a college. Many colleges don't even hold interviews, and others don't put interview notes in students' files. However, at some schools an interview can make a difference between being admitted and not being admitted to the college. You can't change your grades or scores, but a good interview can make you a more attractive admissions prospect. This is especially true if you are applying to a selective school and are not at the top of the list for admission.

When to schedule an interview

It helps to schedule an interview after a campus tour because you are then more familiar with what the college is like and able to ask better questions. You should call rather than write to schedule an interview because you may have to juggle dates to find an interview time, especially in the fall, which is when most high school seniors schedule their interviews. Saturday morning is the most popular time. For very selective schools, it is probably a good idea to schedule an interview as much as two months in advance of your proposed date to visit a college. Because interviewers are so rushed in the fall, interviews in the spring of your junior year or summer before your senior year may be longer and easier to arrange. Try to schedule interviews at schools where you really want to be accepted after you have interviewed at other schools so you will be more experienced with the interviewing process.

Rules for a successful interview

College admissions officers agree that there are certain basic rules that must be followed for a successful interview:

- Be prepared.

- Take your interview confirmation ticket.

- Arrive early for your interview.

- Dress conservatively.

- Introduce anyone who is with you.

- Leave your family and/or friends in the waiting room.

- Participate actively in the interview.

- Be yourself.

- Send a thank-you note after.

How to prepare for the interview

Unless you have read the school brochures and viewbooks from cover to cover or spent considerable time on-line at a Web site, you simply won't have the basic information about a school that you need for an interview. Interviewers are not impressed with students when an entire interview is spent discussing information about the college that the student should have known from doing some reading about the school. It also helps to have toured the campus before your interview so that you have a better feel of the school's atmosphere.

Prepare to answer basic questions. No matter where you interview, the interviewer is likely to ask questions about the type of person you are, your values and goals, and your reasons for wanting to attend the college. If you haven't given some thought to these topics, you may stumble with your answers. Since you may be asked the following questions at every interview, take the time now to write down how you will answer them. There are no right or wrong answers to these questions; however, you want to show interviewers that you have spent some time thinking about these basic questions.

1. Why do you want to attend this college?

_____

_____

_____

_____

_____

_____

_____

_____

_____

_____

2. What are you thinking of as a possible major? Why?

_____

_____

_____

_____

_____

_____

_____

_____

_____

_____

3. What do you see yourself doing in the future? Five years from now? Ten years from now?

_____

_____

_____

_____

_____

_____

_____

_____

_____

4. What are your most important contributions to your high school?

_____

_____

_____

_____

_____

_____

_____

_____

5. How would you describe yourself to a stranger? (Use many adjectives.)

_____

_____

_____

_____

_____

_____

_____

_____

Expect to answer some of these questions. As the interviewer gets to know you better, he or she may ask many questions like the following. Thinking about your answers before will make you feel more relaxed at the interview.

College

1. Why do you want to go to college?

2. Where else are you applying to college?

3. What do you feel you have to offer this college?

4. What do you expect to get out of a college education?

5. What extracurricular activities do you plan to pursue in college?

High School

1. Which subject have you liked best or least in high school?

2. How demanding is your high school?

3. What kind of a student have you been?

4. What is your favorite teacher like?

5. What would you like to change about your high school?

Yourself

1. How would your teachers or friends describe you?

2. What are your greatest strengths or weaknesses?

3. Who are your heroes? Why?

4. What books have you read this year?

5. What extracurricular activity has been most satisfying?

Anticipate some unusual questions. Some interviewers like to see how you can handle something out of the ordinary. How you answer unusual questions is less important than your ability not to be flustered by them. What would you reply to these questions?

1. How would you spend $1 million in twenty-four hours?

2. Would you rather be an elephant or a mouse?

Have some questions of your own. Sometime during the interview the interviewer will ask if you have any questions. You want to ask questions that reveal how seriously you are interested in the school rather than ones that could be answered by reading the college brochure. Ask, "Is it possible to have a double major in psychology and history?" Don't ask, "Is there a psychology department?"

Write down three questions now that you would like to ask at the interview. Then take them with you to the interview in case your mind goes blank.

1. _____

_____

_____

2. _____

_____

_____

3. _____

_____

_____

What to expect

When you arrive at the admissions office for your interview, it may be crowded with other prospective students and their parents. You need to sign in and take a seat. Your interviewer will come into the office and call your name. Stand up at once so the interviewer knows who you are. Greet the interviewer with a handshake and introduce anyone who is with you.

Your interview will last from twenty to forty-five minutes. The length of time is more dependent on the interviewer's schedule than on the way you have impressed the interviewer. It will usually begin with break-the-ice pleasantries like a discussion of your trip to the college. The rest of the interview will be devoted to the interviewer's questions and your questions. At the end of the interview, express your appreciation for the opportunity to learn more about the school. Be sure to learn the interviewer's name, because later you will want to write a letter repeating how you valued the interview and mentioning something that was discussed to remind the interviewer of you.

Alumni interviews

Some selective colleges require alumni interviews. Others strongly recommend alumni interviews. These interviews can take the place of on-campus interviews when it is impossible for students to visit a school. Many students have both on-campus and alumni interviews. Like on-campus interviews, alumni interviews are an opportunity for students to learn more about a college and to put additional information about themselves into their admissions folders. Prepare for these interviews in the same way you do for on-campus interviews.

Prepare a Winning Application

When admissions officers are sitting around a table deciding who to admit, you won't be there to plead your case. You won't be able to explain the success of the club that you started to prevent students from dropping out of high school or that you just missed winning the state golf title. The only thing at the table to tell the admissions officers about you is your application. It has to be filled out in such a way that the admissions officers can clearly see why you are so special that you should be admitted to their college.

Because your application can play an important part in the selection process, especially at selective schools, you want it to do an effective job of presenting your strengths. As part of the application, you want to write an essay that expands your candidacy and choose teachers who will give you good recommendations. In this chapter, you will learn how to fill out college applications, write an essay, and get recommendations from your teachers so that your application gives the message "Admit me" to admissions officers.

Getting an Application

Once you have decided on what schools to apply to, get your applications as soon as possible. Then you can begin to fill some of them out in the summer before your busy senior year begins.

For many schools, applications are now just a few clicks on a mouse away. Many college Web sites offer applications for downloading. Also, many companies offer access to applications for hundreds of colleges. A list of some of the Web sites that have college applications is in Appendix B. Of course you can still get paper applications by calling, e-mailing, or writing to college admissions offices. And you will often find applications included in informational materials colleges send to prospective students.

In the last few years, there has been a move toward applications that can be used to apply to several colleges. Almost 200 colleges accept what is known as the *Common Application*. Some of these schools require supplemental information such as an essay. You can obtain copies of the Common Application at your school's guidance or career office or download it from several Web sites including the National Association of Secondary School Principals Web site at http://nassp.org/services/commapp.htm.

The computer has also made it easier to apply to colleges. No longer is it necessary to complete an application for each school. Hundreds of schools will accept applications on which you fill in common background information only once for all the schools and then complete the sections unique to each school. Depending on the computer service, you can complete such application forms on-line over several sessions or download them to be completed later. The service then typically sends a printed application for each school to you for your review. You can learn more in Appendix B about how to access Web sites offering these services.

Caution: Before you register to use an application system, make sure the colleges to which you are applying accept such applications.

Deciding Which Admissions Option Is Best

There is not a single application deadline for all colleges nor is there just one date by which all students are notified if they have been admitted. Colleges have adopted a variety of admissions options because many students want to know early whether they have been accepted. If you have decided that one college is definitely your first choice, you may want to ask for an early admissions decision if this option is offered by the college. One of the first blanks to fill in on many applications is the box for the admissions option you want.

Regular admissions

The advantage of regular admission is that it has the latest deadlines for application. The disadvantage of this option is that it also has the latest acceptance notification dates. Selective schools usually do not send out this information until early April.

Most students choose to apply to college under the regular admission plan, which requires them to send in their applications by a certain date, usually in late fall or winter. Admissions decisions are then sent out to all candidates on the same date usually in the spring. Some colleges offer only the regular admissions option and do not have any early admissions plans.

Rolling admissions

Many colleges, especially large state universities, admit students on a continuing basis until the freshman class is full. As soon as your application is sent in, the admissions officers begin to process it. How soon you receive notification of admission depends on the school. It could be just a few weeks after you send in your application. Students whose grades and test scores are very close to minimum entrance requirements may have to wait quite a while for a decision. Because students are accepted on a first-come, first-served basis, it is to your advantage to apply early to these schools before the class is filled.

Early decision

If you have a strong high school record and are intent on attending your first-choice college, you should consider applying for early decision. Usually, you apply in November and receive the school's decision in December or January. At that time, you are either accepted or rejected, or action on your application is deferred to the regular admissions deadline.

Each school that offers this admissions option has different rules, so be sure that you understand what is involved. By signing up for early admission, you agree to attend the college if you are accepted. Some schools let students apply to other schools at the same time; however, they must withdraw all other applications if accepted under early decision.

Early action

A few selective schools offer early action, which is similar to early decision. The main difference is that if you are accepted, you have until the regular admissions deadline to decide whether you want to attend. The students applying for this plan are usually very strong candidates.

Decisions on admissions options

Look over the admissions options for each of the colleges to which you are applying for admission. Decide which option you will use for each school. Be sure to study the rules for the early decision option carefully because some schools will not allow you to apply to other colleges under this option. Use the following chart to record the admissions options you have chosen.

Admissions Options Chart

| Colleges | Admissions options | | | |
	Regular	Rolling	Early decision	Early action

Keeping Track of Admissions Deadlines

If you are applying to several colleges, you will find it mind-boggling to keep track of all the different deadlines. It is very difficult to do because individual colleges have different deadlines for when applications, financial aid, high school records, test scores, and teacher recommendation forms are due. Use the following chart to make sure you meet all these deadlines. Be sure to indicate if a form must be *received* or *postmarked* by a deadline. As soon as you get an application, enter all the deadlines on this chart. Then draw a line through each deadline as you meet it.

Application Deadlines Checklist

	Deadlines for submission							
Colleges	**Admissions application**	**Financial aid application**	**Teacher reference forms**	**High school record form**	**ACT or SAT I results**	**SAT II Tests results**	**First semester report form**	**Additional information**

Guidelines for Completing Applications

Fill out your applications early and mail or send them electronically well before the deadlines. This gives the admissions officers a chance to study your applications rather than speed-read them along with all the other applications that were submitted at the last minute. Here are some basic steps that you should follow in filling out your applications whether you are completing them on a computer or a typewriter.

Copy paper applications. Make several copies of an application as soon as you receive it so you have spares for practice.

Read the entire application. Always read the entire application through several times so you clearly understand what information is required in each section.

Read the directions carefully. Never put a mark on a paper application or fill in a computer form before you have read the directions. Then follow them to the letter.

Practice on the copy. Fill out your complete paper application on a copy before filling out the original. This way you will know how to space what you want to say.

Be very neat. Type or use a computer, and avoid excessive use of correction fluid.

Make your copy readable. Use an easy-to-read font in 10 to 12 point type. Avoid using less than single spacing.

Use the space wisely. Stay within the space allotted for your answers. The space indicates how much information the colleges want. If you absolutely must have more space to answer a question, attach an additional information page rather than try to cram your answer into a small space.

Be truthful. You are describing the real you and your actual accomplishments. You want this to agree with what the school record and your recommendations say. It is not necessary, however, to point out your weaknesses.

Pay attention to details. Don't forget to answer any questions. Remember to sign your application.

Proofread your application. Never mail an application until you and at least one other person have carefully edited and proofread it. Watch for spelling and grammar errors. Use a computer spelling check program, if possible.

Photocopy your completed application. This is simple insurance in case it gets misplaced in your home, the mail, or the admissions office.

Completing an Actual Application

Some college applications are a breeze to fill out—no more than a page of general information is required. The more selective the admissions process is at a school, the greater the amount of information you will have to provide. You will also have to write short answers and longer essays. To learn how to fill out an application, fill out the copy of the Common Application provided on the next four pages. Once you have filled out this application, you will find it much easier to fill out others.

Looking at the Common Application

When you look at an actual Common Application, you will see at the top of the first page the list of colleges that use it. Study the list carefully, as one or more of the schools on your final list might use this application. Some of the colleges using this application will want supplementary material that they will tell you about as soon as they receive your application.

Read through the entire application to get a feel for the type of information you need to provide. The Common Application, like other applications, is broken down into several sections requiring different types of information. You are asked to provide the following:

- personal data;

- educational data;

- test information;

- family information;

- academic honors;

- extracurricular, personal, and volunteer activities (including summer);

- work experience; and

- personal statement (essay).

You will notice at once that the written record you made in Chapter 8 of all that you have done in high school will

1998-99 Common Application©

Application for Undergraduate Admission

Member colleges and universities encourage the use of this application. No distinction will be made between it and the college's own form. The accompanying instructions tell you how to complete, copy, and file your application with any one or several of the colleges.

Personal Data

☐ Male
☐ Female

Legal Name: _____ _____ _____ _____
Last/Family   First   Middle (complete)   Jr., etc.

Prefer to be called: _____ (nickname)   Former last name(s) if any: _____

Applying as a ☐ Freshman ☐ Transfer   For the term beginning: _____

Permanent home address: _____
Number and Street

_____ _____ _____ _____
City or Town   State   Country Zip Code + 4 or Postal Code

Is your mailing address for admissions correspondence the same? ☐ Yes

Mailing address: _____ Use from: _____ To: _____
Number and Street

_____ _____ _____ _____
City or Town   State   Country Zip Code + 4 or Postal Code

Phone at mailing address: _____   Phone at permanent address: _____
Include area code   Include area code

E-mail address: _____

Birthdate (mm/dd/yy): _____   ☐ Citizenship: U.S./dual U.S. citizen.   If dual, specify other citizenship: _____

☐ U.S. Permanent resident visa.   Citizen of: _____   ☐ Other citizenship.   Please specify country: _____

If you are not a U.S. citizen and live in the United States, how long have you been in the country? _____ Visa Type: _____

Possible area(s) of academic concentration/major: _____   ☐ Or undecided

Special college or division if applicable: _____

Possible career or professional plans: _____   ☐ Or undecided

Will you be a candidate for financial aid? ☐ Yes ☐ No   If yes, the appropriate form(s) was/will be filed on (mm/dd/yy): _____

The following items are optional: Social Security number, if any: _____   Marital status: _____

Place of birth: _____ _____ _____
City or Town   State   Country

First language, if other than English: _____   Language spoken at home: _____

If you wish to be identified with a particular ethnic group, please check the following:

☐ African American, Black

☐ American Indian, Alaskan Native (Tribal affiliation _____ Enrolled ____)

☐ Asian American   (Country of family's origin _____)   (mm/yy)

☐ Asia (Indian Subcontinent)   (Country _____)

☐ Hispanic, Latino   (Country _____)

☐ Mexican American, Chicano

☐ Native Hawaiian, Pacific Islander

☐ Puerto Rican

☐ White or Caucasian

☐ Other (Specify _____)

1998-99

APP-1

Educational Data

School you now attend: _____   Date of Entry (mm/yy): _____

Address: _____ _____ _____   CEEB/ACT code: _____

Date of secondary graduation (mm/yy): _____   School is ☐ Public   ☐ Private   ☐ Parochial

College counselor: Name: _____   Position: _____

School phone: _____   School fax: _____

List all other secondary schools, including summer schools and programs you have attended beginning with ninth grade.

Name of School	Location (City, State, Zip)	Dates Attended

List all colleges at which you have taken courses for credit and list names of courses taken and grades earned on a separate sheet. Please have an official transcript sent from each institution as soon as possible.

Name of College	Location (City, State, Zip)	Degree Candidate?	Dates Attended
		☐	
		☐	
		☐	

☐ If not currently attending school, please check here.   Describe in detail, on a separate sheet, your activities since last enrolled.

Test Information

Be sure to note the tests required for each institution to which you are applying. The official scores from the appropriate testing agency must be submitted to each institution as soon as possible. Please list your test plans below.

SAT I (or SAT)	Date Taken/ to be taken	

mm/yy   Verbal   Math   mm/yy   Verbal   Math

SAT II Subject Tests (or Achievements)   Date

mm/yy   Subject   Score   mm/yy   Subject   Score   mm/yy   Subject   Score

mm/yy   Subject   Score   mm/yy   Subject   Score   mm/yy   Subject   Score

ACT   Date Taken/ to be taken

mm/yy   English Score   Math Score   Reading Score   Science Score   Composite Score

Test of English as a Foreign Language (TOEFL)   Date Taken/ to be taken

mm/yy   Score

Family

Mother's full name: _____   Father's full name: _____

Is she living? _____   Is he living? _____

Home address if different from yours: Home address if different from yours:

_____   _____

_____   _____

Occupation (describe briefly): _____   Occupation (describe briefly): _____

Name of business or organization: _____   Name of business or organization: _____

College (if any): _____   College (if any): _____

Degree: _____ Year: _____   Degree: _____ Year: _____

Professional or graduate school (if any): _____   Professional or graduate school (if any): _____

Degree: _____ Year: _____   Degree: _____ Year: _____

If not with both parents, with whom do you make your permanent home: _____

Please check if parents are ☐ Married ☐ Separated ☐ Divorced Date: _____ ☐ Other _____
1998-99

APP-2

Please give names and ages of your brothers or sisters. If they have attended college, give the names of the institutions attended, degrees, and approximate dates:

Academic Honors

Briefly describe any scholastic distinctions or honors you have won beginning with ninth grade:

Extracurricular, Personal, and Volunteer Activities (including summer)

Please list your principal extracurricular, community, and family activities and hobbies in the order of their interest to you. Include specific events and/or major accomplishments such as musical instruments played, varsity letters earned, etc. Please mark in the right column those activities you hope to pursue in college. To allow us to focus on the highlights of your activities, please complete this section even if you plan to attach a resume.

Activity	Grade level or post-secondary (p.s.)					Approximate time spent		Positions held, honors won, or letters earned	Do you plan to participate in college?
	9	10	11	12	PS	Hours per week	Weeks per year		
	☐	☐	☐	☐	☐				☐
	☐	☐	☐	☐	☐				☐
	☐	☐	☐	☐	☐				☐
	☐	☐	☐	☐	☐				☐
	☐	☐	☐	☐	☐				☐
	☐	☐	☐	☐	☐				☐
	☐	☐	☐	☐	☐				☐

Work Experience

List any job (including summer employment) you have held during the past three years.

Specific nature of work	Employer	Approximate dates of employment		Approximate no. of hours per week
		From	To	

In the space provided below or on a separate sheet if necessary, please describe which of these activities (extracurricular and personal activities or work experience) has had the most meaning for you, and why.

Personal Statement

This personal statement helps us become acquainted with you as an individual in ways different from courses, grades, test scores, and other objective data. Please write an essay (250-500 words) on a topic of your choice or on one of the options listed below. You may attach your essay on separate sheets (same size, please).

1. Evaluate a significant experience or achievement that has special meaning to you.

2. Discuss some issue of personal, local, national, or international concern and its importance to you.

3. Indicate a person who has had a significant influence on you, and describe that influence.

I understand that: (1) If I am an Early Action or Early Decision candidate, I must attach a letter with this application, or complete the college's reqired ED form, notifying that college of my intent, and (2) it is my responsibility to report any changes in my schedule to the colleges to which I am applying.

My signature below indicates that all information in my application is complete, factually correct, and honestly presented.

Signature _____   Date _____

These colleges are committed to administer all educational policies and activities without discrimination on the basis of race, color, religion, national or ethnic origin, age, handicap, or sex. The admissions process at private undergraduate institutions is exempt from the federal regulation implementing Title IX of the Education Amendments of 1972.

1998-99

APP-4

make it very easy for you to fill out the information sections of the application. However, before you begin to fill out the application, think carefully about the image you wish to present to the admissions officers. Is it that of a serious student; an accomplished artist, musician, actor, or writer; an athlete; or an all-around student? Since you can't use every detail in your written record, use the ones that support how you want the admissions officers to see you.

Completing the personal data section

The first part of this section is largely devoted to facts that will help the school identify you. Remember to use the same name as you did for registering for the admissions tests. If you use a nickname instead of a first name, be sure to use that name on your application. This is the name that you want to find on the door to your room and in the freshman photo book when you arrive on campus. In this section and all the other sections, be sure to fill in every item that applies to you.

Possible area of academic concentration / major. Before you fill in your choice, be sure that you can answer "yes" to these questions:

1. Does the college offer that area of academic concentration/major? (Many schools do not have prelaw, premedicine, or business majors. Check the catalog.) Yes No

2. Did I demonstrate strength in this area in high school? (In other words, don't choose to concentrate or major in French if you have all C grades in that subject.) Yes No

3. Does the choice of a certain academic concentration/major affect my admission chances at a state school? (Some areas like computer science are very popular, so admission with this academic concentration/ major can be more competitive.) Yes No

Special college or division. Most students will leave this line blank. But look in a catalog if you are interested in a field like mining, art, nursing, agriculture, engineering, or music to see if there are special colleges or divisions for these fields within a school.

Possible career or professional plans. College admissions officers do not expect you to know what you will be doing in four years, so an "undecided" answer is perfectly acceptable here. Also, don't choose a career or profession that is incompatible with your high school grades and interests.

Financial aid. You will learn all about financial aid in Chapter 13. Check "Yes" if you need financial aid. Most colleges do not consider financial need in making admissions decisions. Find out the financial aid deadlines to make sure you file your form on time.

Optional items. There is no reason not to fill in this section. If you are a member of a minority, it may be to your advantage to describe yourself, as schools like to have diverse student bodies.

Completing the educational data section

On the Common Application as well as most other applications, this is a very simple section to complete. The CEEB/ACT code number is the same number you used in registering for college entrance tests. Your college counselor is usually your guidance counselor unless a different person handles this task at your school. Fill in all the blanks in this section as a college may need to contact your school for more information about you.

Completing the test information section

Besides listing your scores on admissions tests that you have taken, be sure to give the dates of tests you are yet to take or retake. Also, note that you must request that the testing agencies send your official scores to the school, and there are deadlines for when schools must have these scores.

Completing the family section

The family information section lets colleges know what your family background is. It also does one other thing: It lets the colleges know where members of your family went to college. If your parents, brothers, or sisters happened to attend a college to which you are applying, this may give you an admissions advantage. The more selective the college, the more important the alumni connection is in the admissions process.

Listing your academic honors

Here is one section where reading directions counts. Note you are being asked to list only *academic* honors, not other honors like prom queen or most valuable player. And you are also being asked to start your list with honors won beginning in the ninth grade, so put your honors in the correct chronological order. Since the space is limited, go back to Chapter 8 and choose only the most important academic honors from your listing of honors, awards, and prizes. If you have won the same honor more than once, list the honor followed by the years it was won—for example, High Honor Roll—9, 10, 11.

Listing extracurricular, personal, and volunteer activities

One of the important factors that colleges consider in deciding whether to admit students is their participation in extracurricular activities. So fill in this section carefully, being sure to select your most significant accomplishments outside of the classroom. Look at the list of extracurricular activities that you made in Chapter 8 in order to complete this section. Also notice that the colleges want to hear about family activities and hobbies that interest you. So here is the place to mention you are a gourmet cook, needlepoint expert, computer programmer, or skilled car mechanic. It is also the spot to list significant travel experiences such as a summer abroad. Again, it is important to read and follow the directions. List the activities in the order of their interest to you.

Because space is limited, you should realize that the colleges don't want a long list of activities that are not important to you. This is also obvious because they are asking how much time you devote to each activity in a week. You won't need to list any club that meets only once or twice in a semester, but you will certainly want to list any club in which you hold an office or are actively involved in some way or a sport that requires some of your time each week. If you don't find the space sufficient for listing all of your activities, indicate that you have attached a resume. You can then complete your listings on the extra page, which should also have your name and address on it.

When filling out this list, you want to make sure that you give specific rather than general information for the activity column. Don't use a broad term like *music*. Instead, use narrower terms like *pep band* or *concert orchestra*. Make sure what you write in the "positions held, honors won, or letters earned" column clearly reflects the part you have played in an activity. This is not an easy task in the limited space provided; using abbreviations like MVP for most valuable player can help. Also, you can use two lines for an activity, if appropriate. See how much information the following sample entries for this column give:

Extracurricular, Personal, and Volunteer Activities (Including Summer)

Please list your principal extracurricular, community, and family activities and hobbies in the order of their interest to you. Include specific events and/or major accomplishments such as musical instruments played, varsity letters earned, etc. Please mark in the right column those activities you hope to pursue in college. To allow us to focus on the highlights of your activities, complete this section even if you plan to attach a resume.

Activity	Grade level or post-secondary (p.s.)					Approximate time spent		Positions held, honors won, or letters earned	Do you plan to participate in college?
	9	10	11	12	P.S.	Hours per week	Weeks per year		
Competitive tennis	x	x	x	x		16	40	State rank—top 10 Regional rank—top 25	x
Varsity tennis	x	x	x	x		14	10	Cpt., MVP—12 Letters—10, 11, 12	x
Student council		x		x		1	36	President—12	x
Big Brothers and Big Sisters			x	x		2	50	Tutor and coach	x
School newspaper	x	x				5	36	Sports editor—10 Copy editor—9	
TV–Brain Game Team			x	x		7		State runner-up—11	
Electric guitar	x	x	x	x		3	40	Rock band—9–12	

Don't worry about explaining your activities as fully as you want in this section. In the section at the bottom of the page, you have an opportunity to discuss in greater detail either an activity or work experience that has had the most meaning for you.

Completing the work experience section

Besides considering grades, test scores, and extracurricular activities colleges also consider your work experience when making admissions decisions. You may not have held a steady job, but colleges want to hear about temporary jobs like babysitting and yard work. Begin this section with your most recent job. If you need additional space to list all the jobs that you have held, attach an extra page or put this information on the extra page for activities. Be sure to be specific in describing your jobs.

Writing about your activities

When you write about the activity or work experience that has had the most meaning for you, your application becomes more than a basic information sheet. You are letting the admissions officers know why you use your time in a particular way. Consider this brief discussion or any question that you are asked to answer on an application as a mini essay. Write with care just like you would on an essay. Stay within the allotted space, as the colleges are asking for short answers.

Writing the personal statement or essay

If you write the most fabulous essay that grips the imagination of every admissions officer at a college, will it improve your chances of admission? Yes. Writing a poor essay with spelling and grammar errors can also hurt your chances. When colleges ask for you to write an essay or personal statement as the Common Application does, the essay does play a part in the admissions process but it certainly isn't the major factor in determining whether or not you will be admitted.

The point of the college application essay, according to Paul Thiboutot, Dean of Admissions at Carleton College, is to help the admissions officers gain some insight into the personal aspect of the candidate—how the candidate thinks and uses his or her time. Essays should also show substance and good writing. So use the essay or essays you write to expand your candidacy beyond grades, test scores, and lists of accomplishments to show the person you are. Also use your essay or essays to establish yourself as a good writer capable of clearly expressing your thoughts while using correct grammar and spelling. In other words, write an essay that would receive an A in your English class. Before you begin to write your essay, you may find it helpful to read the essays of successful college applicants in order to learn what is expected of you. You will find a list of suggested books in Appendix A.

Guidelines for writing an essay

Whether an essay is assigned or you have to choose a topic, there are certain guidelines that you must follow.

Write it yourself. Ask your English teacher, friends, or parents to make suggestions about topics. It's acceptable to show them your finished essay, but don't let them rewrite your paper because it won't sound like you, and admissions officers will notice.

Give yourself time. Start early enough so you have sufficient time to write, rewrite, and proofread all of your essays.

Stick to the topic. Colleges want to see how all their applicants discuss a stated topic or answer the same question.

Be organized. Follow the same steps that you do in writing essays for your classes. Have an introduction, body, and conclusion in your essay.

Use your own language. Admissions officers are not impressed by fancy words taken from a thesaurus.

Add dimension to your application. Don't repeat what you have already said in the information sections of your application.

Keep your essays brief. Stay within the space limit. Extra pages do not impress admissions officers.

Be careful with humor. Humor can add life to your essay. Make sure it reveals you as a clever, not shallow person.

Be original. Don't quote well-known phrases that thousands of applicants have used before you. Forget quoting Robert Frost, Martin Luther King Jr., and William Shakespeare.

Be specific. Every year applicants write about such generalities as wanting world peace, obtaining a liberal arts education, and expanding their horizons. Narrow your focus to specifics like teaching your blind brother to swim, your small role with a major opera company, and delivering pizzas on time.

Edit and proofread. Check once, twice, three times that what you have written is correct. Have others edit and proofread your essays, too.

Adapt essays for reuse. One essay cannot possibly be used on all applications because few questions and essay topics are identical. This doesn't mean, however, that you can't modify an essay for use on a different application.

Always write optional essays. This is just one more chance to let admissions officers learn more about you and to set yourself apart from other candidates.

Evaluating an essay

Carefully read the following essay, which was written to discuss the second topic on the Common Application personal statement about some issue of personal, local, or national concern and its importance to you. Then use the chart that follows it to evaluate it.

A significant problem facing my generation is the aging of the United States population. Today there are nearly ten times as many people over sixty-five as there were in 1900. Never before has the possibility existed of a society having as many older people as young people. This is the condition forecast for the United States in 2040 when my generation reaches sixty-five.

Long before my generation reaches sixty-five, we will have to face some of the problems of an aging population. The cost of providing a long and comfortable retirement for so many people has already created serious financial problems in the Social Security system. All programs for older Americans now constitute approximately 25 percent of the federal budget. The elderly's share of the budget could soar to over 60 percent by 2040 if the current programs remain unchanged. This would cause financial problems of disastrous proportions. Even though a large amount of money is now being spent on older people, almost one-third of the elderly live in poverty or near poverty.

The problems of an aging population are not limited to the financial sphere. Older people have more health problems than younger people. More hospitals, nursing homes, and medical personnel will be required as the population continues to grow older. The percentage of people in the work force will decline as the population ages. A shortage of workers may occur.

Not only must my generation solve some of these significant problems of an aging population, we must also find a useful role for older people in the United States in order to make our own futures bright. As individuals we can begin by finding ways to improve the relationships between young and old in our own families. As a group we can work for the implementation of policies that encourage a longer worklife and a shorter retirement.

Grading the essay. Give the essay a grade from A to F in each of the following areas. Then give it an overall grade.

Organization: _____   Originality: _____

Narrowness of focus: _____   Grammar: _____

Language: _____   Overall grade: _____

Writing your own essay

Use the space on the application to write your own essay on one of the three topics. When you are finished writing the essay, edit and proofread it using the questions in Chapter 5. Then give your essay a grade using the following criteria. The sample essay you just read would have received a C from an admissions officer at a selective school.

Organization: _____   Originality: _____

Narrowness of focus: _____   Grammar: _____

Language: _____   Overall grade: _____

Getting the Recommendations You Need

When you fill out a college application, you tell your story about what you have done in high school. When teachers write recommendations for you, they reinforce what you have said plus tell about how they think you will handle college. Recommendations can improve or hurt your chances for admission, so it is very important to choose teachers who will write the best recommendations for you.

What teachers will be asked about you

To help colleges make admissions decisions, teachers are asked to rate or describe your academic performance, intellectual promise, and personal qualities. Many colleges use a checklist similar to the one in Chapter 3 and on the Common Application:

Ratings

Compared to other students in his or her entire secondary school class, how do you rate this student in terms of:

No basis		Below Average	Average	Good (above average)	Very Good (well above average)	Excellent (top 10%)	One of the top few encountered in my career
	Creative, original thought						
	Motivation						
	Self-confidence						
	Independence, initiative						
	Intellectual ability						
	Academic achievement						
	Written expression of ideas						
	Effective class discussion						
	Disciplined work habits						
	Potential for growth						

Instead of using a ratings checklist colleges may ask teachers to answer questions like the following:

- What can you tell us about the applicant's intellectual qualities and academic work?

- What are the first words that come to your mind to describe this applicant's character?

- What is the quality of the applicant's performance in extracurricular, community, or work activities?

- How do you think this applicant would do on personal and academic grounds at this college?

Almost all recommendation forms ask recommenders how long they have known applicants as well as what subjects they have taught applicants. They may also be asked what grades they have given the applicant. In choosing a teacher to write a recommendation, you should consider how the teacher would complete the ratings form and answer the preceding questions.

How to select teachers to write recommendations

Obviously you want to select teachers who will write positive, if not glowing, recommendations for you. A selected teacher should have taught you recently in an academic class. It is also a good idea to choose teachers from different areas if you are asked to submit more than one recommendation. If you have listed a major, it makes sense to choose a teacher in that area.

Write down on the following chart the names of at least four teachers you may want to have write recommendations for you. Answer the questions about each teacher with a "Yes" or "No."

Choose the teachers who had the most "Yes" answers to write your recommendations. Surprisingly, your favorite teachers may not be the ones you choose. Because it takes time to write recommendations, you may want to ask more than one teacher to do this for you. If you are convinced that one teacher is the best choice, you might suggest that the teacher write a recommendation on school stationery and make copies of it.

Evaluating Recommenders

Questions	Teachers				
1. Is the teacher a good writer? (English teachers usually are.)					
2. Have you had a class from this teacher recently? (It's been a long time since you studied freshman biology.)					
3. Does this teacher really know you?					
4. Has this teacher worked as a sponsor or coach of one of your extra-curricular activities?					
5. Does this teacher like you?					
6. Will this teacher write a strong recommendation for you? (If uncertain, ask the teacher.)					
7. Will this teacher complete and mail the recommendation on time?					
8. Did this teacher attend the college that you want to attend? (It helps if the teacher knows the school.)					
Total number of "Yes" answers:					

How to help your teachers write your recommendations

The earlier in your senior year you ask teachers to write recommendations for you, the fewer the number of forms they will be busy completing for other students. Once a teacher has agreed to write a recommendation, ask for a conference to talk about your college plans. Take to this meeting recommendation forms and stamped, addressed envelopes. You also should hand the teacher a letter giving deadline dates for each recommendation and a description of what you have been doing in high school. This background information will help the teacher remember your achievements when writing the recommendation. Complete the following exercise so you will know what to say in your letter:

Dear _____

I enjoy(ed) being in your _____

course(s) because _____

_____

_____.

I have been most enthusiastic about courses in _____

_____ because

_____.

In college, I hope to study _____ because _____

_____

_____.

To assist you in completing my recommendation form(s), I want to tell you about some of my activities during high school. My favorite extracurricular activity has been _____

_____.

Participation in this activity has included doing such things as _____

_____

_____

_____ .

I have also participated in these activities: _____

_____

_____

Outside of school my principal interests have been _____

_____

_____

_____ .

The college deadline(s) for receiving these recommendations is (are):

(college)   (deadline)

_____   _____

_____   _____

I appreciate your help in writing this (these) recommendation(s) for me.

Sincerely,

_____

Evaluation by the college advisor or guidance counselor

Besides giving recommendation forms to teachers, you will need to give a school report form to your college advisor, who usually is your guidance counselor. This form asks about your class rank and often asks the counselor to rate certain characteristics on a checklist and to answer questions similar to those on the teacher recommendation forms. Because the counselor is rating you, it is to your advantage to have shared your college plans with him or her. It is also a good idea to check over your transcript with the counselor to make sure it is accurate in every way, as this is the record of your grades and activities that will be sent to the colleges. Be sure to thank your counselor for completing the school report form in a letter. You may also want to include in the letter the same background information that you gave to the teachers writing recommendations for you.

Sending extra recommendations

Colleges usually ask you to submit one, two, or three recommendations. There is no reason to submit extra recommendations unless they add dimension to your application. It is a good idea to submit a recommendation from a coach or an art, music, or other special subjects teacher if you have special talents that you want to pursue at college. Most colleges are looking for applicants who are exceptional in one area. This could give you an edge in the admissions process. For the same reason, you may also want to talk to college coaches, music conductors, and others since they can put in a good word for you at the admissions office. You can also submit a recommendation from a boss or someone with whom you have worked as a volunteer. Recommendations from political leaders and prominent alumni have no value unless these people know you well.

Supporting Your Application

You have probably heard about students sending such intriguing items as newspaper articles about themselves, fabulous desserts for the admissions officers, and tapes of original operas along with their applications. Extra materials can help you be admitted if they add something to your application by showing a skill or talent not documented thoroughly. One caution: Make sure that a college wants to receive extra materials. Some colleges even tell you how to submit them. Be careful about submitting gimmicks like T-shirts and cartoons, as the admissions officers may not find them clever. Look over this list of materials that are often sent to colleges and decide if any of them might enhance your application:

- photographs or slides of artworks

- artwork—sculpture, paintings, pottery, jewelry

- photographs—if you are a photographer

- tapes of solo music performances

- tapes of original music compositions

- newspaper stories you have written

- newspaper stories of an *outstanding,* not routine, accomplishment

- samples of excellent poetry or short stories

- published materials

- computer programs you have created

- videos of athletic, musical, or theatrical performances

Updating your application

If you send your application in early, exciting accomplishments like winning first place in debate in your state, getting the lead in the senior play, or having a children's book published can happen. Since any one of these or similar activities could improve your chances of admission, you want colleges to which you are applying to know about them. Some schools provide a form that you can use to list new information. Or you can send the information on a sheet of paper that also tells when you are applying for admission and gives your name, address, and Social Security number.

Completing the Final Steps

Reread your application immediately after completing it. Then put it aside and read it again the next day to make a final check for errors. Finally, copy your application and mail it. If the college will not be sending you a postcard saying that the application has been received, have the post office send a return receipt request along with the application so you know that it reached the college.

Find Out About Financial Aid

Money! Money! Money! The cost of college continues to increase. Some private schools cost astronomical sums, and even most state schools are expensive. Students and their parents or guardians tend to focus on the high cost of college and not on the many resources available to pay for a college education. In the real world, eight of ten students are eligible for some kind of help with college bills.

Although there are billions of dollars of financial aid available each year, it is not simply handed out with college applications. Instead, students and their parents or guardians must find out where the money is and then apply for it. It takes considerable research. Appendices A and B present lists of financial aid books and Web sites that can be used to open the doors for students to attend college. For a good starting point, read the free booklet *Student Guide: Financial Aid from the U.S. Department of Education.*

In this chapter, you will find out more about what college costs, the types of aid that are available, and how to go about obtaining financial aid. This chapter will get you started in the search for the financial aid you need. The first step is to determine the cost of your college education.

What Will Your College Education Cost?

How much your education costs obviously depends on where you go to college. The difference in cost between a community college and an Ivy League school is enormous. However, you don't want to rule out applying to a school just because of its cost. If you qualify for certain financial aid packages, you may find it no more expensive to go to Harvard or Princeton than to attend a state-supported school.

In Chapter 10, you made a rough estimate of what several colleges you were considering would cost based only on tuition and room and board. To get a more accurate picture of costs at individual colleges, add such expenses as books and supplies, fees, transportation, and personal expenses. You can get information about the cost of these items from college guidebooks and Web pages or directly from the financial aid offices of colleges.

Personal expenses

Because personal expenses vary considerably from student to student, you should figure out what your current personal expenses are rather than using a college's estimate for an average student. This will give you a more realistic budget. Use the following chart to compute your current monthly expenditures. Then multiply by the number of months you will be in school to get your personal expenses for a year in college:

Clothing   _____

Personal care (toiletries)   _____

Telephone (remember long distance)   _____

Entertainment   _____

Tapes and CDs _____

Snacks _____

Restaurants _____

Automobile (if applicable) _____

Laundry and cleaners _____

Other _____

Total monthly expenses $ _____

Total yearly expenses $ _____

Estimated college costs. Fill in the following chart to establish what your costs will be at the colleges to which you are applying for admission:

Colleges	Estimated costs						
	Tuition and fees	Housing	Meals	Books and supplies	Transportation (to and from school)	Personal expenses	Total

How Much Financial Aid Can You Expect?

First of all, you need to understand how financial aid is awarded. When students apply for aid using the Free Application for Federal Student Aid (FAFSA) after January 1 of their senior year, an analysis of the student's family's financial situation is done with a federal formula. Within a month or so and sooner for electronic applications, a Student Aid Report (SAR) is sent out telling how much the student and his or her family are expected to pay toward the cost of attending college. This is called the Expected Family Contribution (EFC), and families are expected to pay this amount at any college their children attend.

Estimating the family contribution

Fortunately, you and your family do not have to wait until you receive your Student Aid Report to know what your Expected Family Contribution will be. Worksheets can help you make a rough estimate of this amount. These worksheets can be found in books on financial aid published by the College Board, ACT, Peterson's, and Octameron Press (see Appendix A) and on the World Wide Web at several sites (see Appendix B). Also, computer software, available at many high schools, can be used to make this estimate.

Estimating the amount of financial aid

Once you know what your Expected Family Contribution is, you will have a good idea of whether you will need additional money to attend a specific college. Note the following examples for a family that is expected to pay $8,000 toward college costs:

Total cost of attendance at college A	$12,000
Minus Expected Family Contribution	− 8,000
Financial need	$ 4,000
Total cost of attendance at college B	$ 8,000
Minus Expected Family Contribution	− 8,000
Financial need	0

Where Does Aid Money Come From?

Most of the money students receive for financial aid comes from the federal government, state governments, and the college's own resources, with the lion's share coming from the federal government. Some colleges have much more money available for financial aid than others. The basic types of aid that students receive are grants, loans, and employment. You may receive just one type of aid or some combination of the three types of financial aid.

Grants do not have to be repaid

For students, grants are the best possible source of financial aid, as they do not have to be repaid. The federal government, state governments, and colleges have grant programs. Most grants are awarded on the basis of need. Scholarships can also be included in this category even though they are often based on achievement as well as need. Scholarships can be obtained from an amazing number of sources.

Although there are many grants available, the federal government provides the most financial aid in this category through Pell Grants and Federal Supplemental Educational Opportunity Grants (FSEOGs).

Pell Grants. All students who are applying for financial aid should apply for Pell Grants because schools do not usually put together financial aid packages for applicants until they know whether the applicants are eligible for Pell Grants. By legislation, this type of grant is available only to undergraduates who meet a certain standard of need. The amount of money available for Pell Grants varies, as Congress determines the funding each year. If you meet the need requirement for this grant, you will receive aid.

Federal Supplemental Educational Opportunity Grants. This government grant program, which is administered by colleges, is for those students with the greatest financial need. Since each college receives only a certain amount of money for these grants, it is a good idea to apply early before the money runs out. Pell Grant recipients are given priority in receiving this grant.

State programs. Every state has its own grant and scholarship programs. The programs are based on both need and scholastic achievement. There are also some programs for students who want to pursue careers in certain areas like teaching or health care as well as programs for the children of veterans. In some cases, it is necessary to take competitive examinations to get this aid. Students usually have to be residents of the state and attend college within the state to get financial aid from a state program. You can find out about these programs from your counselor or the state's higher education agency.

College programs. Colleges have their own resources that allow them to provide scholarships and grants. You will have to check with each college about what is available.

Loans have to be repaid

While loans help you get an education, they can also mean a tremendous debt burden in the future. When you graduate or leave school, you have to start repaying your college loans. On certain loans you even have to start paying interest while you are in school. Some loans are reduced if you join the military or do some type of public service. Repayment may also be delayed if you go to graduate school or serve in the military, Peace Corps, or Vista. Loans like the following ones play a big part in most students' financial aid packages.

Stafford student loans. This is the major loan program at most colleges. In the Direct Loan Program, the funds are lent to you directly by the U.S. government. In the Federal Family Education Loan Program, the funds for your loan come from banks, credit unions, and other lenders. In the subsidized versions of these loans, which are based on need, no interest is due until you leave school. You do not have to have need to qualify for an unsubsidized loan, but you have to pay interest while you are in college. There are limits on the amount of money that can be borrowed each year in all Stafford loan programs as well as a limit on the total amount that can be borrowed by an undergraduate.

Perkins loans. The federal government provides the money for these low-interest loans for students with exceptional financial need, and the colleges act as the lenders. There are limits to the amount of money that can be borrowed.

PLUS loans. These loans are taken out by parents—not students. It is not necessary to show financial need to get one of these loans which are made by the government and by a variety of lending agencies. However, parents or guardians generally are required to pass a credit check. Repayment starts sixty days after the money is received.

Consolidation loans. A consolidation loan is designed to help student and parent borrowers simplify loan repayment by allowing them to consolidate several types of federal student loans into one loan. The interest rate may be lower than that on one or more of their other loans.

State loans. State governments also offer a wide variety of loan programs.

College loans. Colleges offer loans to students from their own resources.

Private loans. Many lending agencies, employers, and organizations offer low-interest educational loans.

Employment is helping yourself

Work-study programs. Colleges administer work-study programs with money that is largely from the federal government, although some state governments also have work-study programs.

These jobs are usually on the college campus, but they can also be with nonprofit organizations. Students work from ten to twenty hours a week for at least minimum wage. Jobs can range from food handler to research assistant to an "America Reads" tutor. Eligibility for work-study programs is based on need and availability of funds. Besides the government work-study programs, many colleges also offer their own employment programs.

AmeriCorps. The AmeriCorps program lets students work before, during, or after college for minimum wage and receive financial credits that can be used at any school or to pay federal student loans. The federal government provides most of the funding, but students are hired by states and nonprofit organizations. Most jobs are related to education, human services, the environment, and other "do good" work.

How Do You Get Financial Aid?

Because applying for financial aid can be quite confusing, begin this process by talking to your guidance counselor or college advisor at your high school. These people know what financial aid programs are available and how to apply for them. All college financial aid offices also have counselors who are willing to talk to you in the office or answer questions on the phone. Whenever you have questions from about how to fill out forms to about where to find aid, talk to people in your high school guidance or career office or in the financial aid office of a college. You need their expert advice. Don't try to do this by yourself.

The first step—applying for government and college aid

Since most financial aid money is based on the Free Application for Federal Student Aid (FAFSA), it only makes sense to fill out this application first. You can get this form at your high school guidance or career office or the financial aid office of a college. Cybersurfers can download a copy. When you fill in this form you are applying for the following financial aid programs:

- most federal student financial aid programs

- most state scholarship and grant programs

- college financial aid programs except for schools that have their own financial aid forms

You can't send FAFSA forms in before January 1 of the year you are applying to college, but you want to get the forms after they come out in November or December and send them in as close to January 1 as possible because some aid is dispensed on a first-come, first-served basis.

It takes about three hours to fill in one of these forms. You give information about the size of your family, debt, education expenses, and unusual expenses as well as your own and your family's incomes and assets. Fill this form out very carefully, as any errors or omissions will only delay the processing of your application. Be sure to make copies of this form before mailing it with a return receipt requested to a need analysis service or sending it electronically.

College financial aid applications. It is important for you to remember that colleges have a great number of financial aid programs that are funded with their own money. Besides filling out the FAFSA form, you may have to submit an application for financial aid to many colleges to which you are applying for admission. More than 300 schools use the PROFILE form, which requires you and your family to answer more questions about your financial situation. It is available at high schools and college financial aid offices as well as on-line at the College Board Web site. Some colleges have their own aid applications.

State financial aid applications. While most states use the FAFSA form, a few require students to submit supplemental applications. Again it is a good idea to submit these applications well before the deadlines, as colleges run out of aid money.

The second step—looking for more financial aid

Unfortunately, you don't find out what your expected family contribution will be until some time after January 1. And you don't find out what your financial aid package will be at a college until after January 1 and after you have been admitted to the school. By the time you have all this information, it is often too late to get more money. So you should explore the following options for getting more money early in your senior year if your own estimates indicate that you will need financial aid.

The military. You probably have heard of ROTC programs and the military academies; there are hundreds of other programs funded by the military. All of these programs require some military service. You will find excellent suggestions in the American Legion's publication *Need a Lift*, which is described in Appendix A.

Cooperative education. Under this program sponsored by companies and the federal government, you combine your college studies with an off-campus job. Some company programs are so generous that they will completely pay for your education. There are two basic work and earn patterns: attending school mornings and working afternoons or vice versa and alternating attending school for a semester and working a semester. Unfortunately, not all schools have these programs and some programs are very competitive.

Cost-cutters. Think of living at home and attending a local college for one or more years. Try to cut your time in college by getting college credits for doing well on Advanced Placement (AP) and College-level Examination Program tests. Think of ways to cut your college budget such as buying only used books, having no car, limiting your social life, or living in cheaper quarters. In addition, you and your family should investigate innovative state and college tuition plans, IRAs, and the tax credits the government gives families who have children in college.

Scholarships. Scholarships that you win become part of your financial aid package. They do not reduce your family contribution unless they exceed the amount of financial aid that you are offered. However, the more scholarships you receive, the less loan money you have to repay. Start your scholarship search in your own high school's guidance or career office to see what is available in your community. This is your best resource. Next, check to see what is available at colleges to which you are applying for admission. Finally, look for scholarships in college guidebooks and on-line (see Appendices A and B). Be sure to look for organizations that sponsor scholarships that are especially appropriate for you because of your background. Investigate the following areas:

_____ school clubs (4-H, Deca)

_____ parents' employers

_____ parents' unions

_____ parents' clubs (civic, fraternal)

_____ your employers (newspapers, fast food companies)

_____ religious affiliation

_____ parents' military service

_____ sports scholarships

_____ special talent schol- arships (art, music)

_____ professional organi- zations in career area (accounting,

health, education, engineering)

_____ nationality

_____ minority status

_____ disability

Caution: Avoid organizations that charge fees for schol- arship searches. The same information is available in books and on the Internet.

Putting together a financial aid package

Once the financial aid office at a college receives the figures on your expected family contribution plus a list of some of the other financial aid that you are eligible for, the office staff is ready to put together a financial aid package that meets your needs. You should be aware that some colleges using their own need formulas often increase the amount of money that families are expected to contribute.

No two colleges will develop the same financial aid package for you. The first money that goes into the package is money from Pell Grants and state programs. Then money from other federal programs and state and college programs plus any money that you have acquired from scholarships are placed in the package. You learn about your financial aid package in an award letter from each college. You have the option of rejecting part of this package. There are also deadlines for accepting the package.

If you find that you need more money after receiving your financial aid package, talk to the college about increasing your aid—it could happen. Many schools discover they have more money for aid when students who are offered aid decide not to enroll. When you need more money, you should also find out if the college or a local bank has any tuition budgeting plans or loan plans that could help you.

What Are the Guideposts for Financial Planning?

Dreaming about going to college is fine, but obtaining the financial aid you need requires effort on your part. Make your aid seeking easier by following these guideposts:

- Begin your search for financial aid early in your senior year.

- Fill in all financial aid forms carefully.

- Apply as early as possible for all forms of financial aid.

- Take advantage of the help your parents or guardians, high school guidance or career counselors, and college financial aid counselors can give you.

Deal Effectively with College Acceptance and Rejection Notices

Fat envelopes, full of information, usually mean that you have been admitted to a college. And believe it or not, most students actually are admitted to the schools that are their first or second choices.

More than likely you will have the pleasant task of deciding which college to attend from several that have sent you acceptance notices. In this chapter, you will find out what to do if there are no acceptance notices in the mail and you will learn what a waiting list is and how to choose a college to attend.

What If You Are Rejected?

If your final list of colleges has some schools in the sure admissions category, you should receive some acceptance letters even if you also receive a few rejections. It can be incredibly difficult to face your friends and family when you have not been admitted to your first- or even second-choice school. Also, you may feel devastated and inclined to keep saying to yourself, "If only I had done this or that." Perhaps it will help a little to know that most students after a few weeks at the colleges where they actually enroll wonder why they weren't their first choices all along.

If you fail to be accepted at a Harvard, Yale, Stanford, or other equally selective school, remember that 80 percent to almost 90 percent of those who apply are also rejected and that the admissions officers of these schools admit that many who are rejected are capable of doing excellent work. Whether a student is rejected by a state-supported university or a very selective school, it is very important for him or her to handle rejection in a positive manner and to work for success at the school in which he or she enrolls.

The possibility of transferring

You always have the possibility of transferring to another college after attending a school for a year if you do not feel it is the right one for you. You become an improved candidate for admission to a college that you applied to earlier when you receive good grades and demonstrate that you can handle college work. Admission for a transfer student is based more on college work than on what the student did in high school. It is far easier to transfer to a school from which quite a few students drop out during their freshman year than to transfer to a very selective school that has few slots for transfer students.

Deciding to appeal rejection

Mistakes can be made. If you have all the qualifications for admission to a school, especially a state-supported school, and are rejected, you should ask for a review of your admissions file. Another reason for asking for a review is having done something after you applied that would make you a more attractive candidate for admission. Improving your grades substantially during your senior year, significantly raising your SAT I or ACT scores, or winning a very important award are examples. Talk to your guidance counselor about whether you should appeal a rejection. Some colleges admit a number of the students appealing rejection while others rarely change admissions decisions.

Facing rejection from all colleges

Students receive only rejection notices when they have not carefully selected the colleges to which they apply. There are colleges within every state that accept all high school graduates. These colleges usually have later deadlines for application than do the more selective schools. So it is possible for most students, even at a late date, to find a college that will admit them. If you have received rejections from all the colleges you applied to, discuss with your parents and counselors how to find colleges that will not only admit you but also meet your needs. Explore other options like waiting a year and then reapplying to colleges.

What If You Are Placed on a Waiting List?

Being placed on a college's waiting list means that the college will admit you if not enough students who were admitted decide to attend. Colleges want to have a full freshman class and will keep admitting students from the waiting list until they do. At some schools, this can mean that students will not know whether they are accepted or rejected until very late in the summer.

What to do about being placed on a college's waiting list only matters if you strongly want to attend that college. If you do, stay on the waiting list but also accept a college that has admitted you—there is no guarantee that you will be accepted from the waiting list. You can call the college admissions office and find out what your chances are of being admitted. You also should write a letter to the college saying how much you still want to attend and giving any new information that might enhance your admissions prospects. It may help to have a teacher or counselor write a letter, too.

How Will You Choose a College to Attend?

More students than you might imagine have the problem of deciding which college to attend, as many are admitted to more than one college. This can be a difficult decision with parents, teachers, and friends all pushing for different schools. The final decision must be yours, and you should devote some time to making it.

If you are in the position of having to decide which college to attend, review the literature of the different colleges and then consider again the factors in Chapter 10 that made you choose to apply to those colleges. Then rate each of these factors *excellent*, *good*, *average*, or *poor* for each college and assign an overall rating to each college. Most students also have to add the factor of cost into their decision.

	Colleges			
Selection factors				
Location				
College environment				
Academic offerings and facilities				
Overall rating				

Considering the cost

All financial aid packages, even those for the same amounts, are not equal. Packages that offer more money in grants and scholarships are more attractive than those that offer more in loans. Use the following cost considerations chart to compare costs of the colleges that have admitted you.

	Colleges			
Cost considerations				
Total cost				
Grants				
Scholarships				
Loans				
Work-study				
Family contribution				

Once you have compared costs, you can visit or contact the financial aid offices at the different colleges to discuss your financial aid options.

Making your final decision

After you have been admitted to a college, the college may invite you to visit. Go if you can, stay in a dorm, visit classes, and wander around the school. There is no better way to test if a school feels right for you.

Then when you are back home, weigh all the factors and choose the school that seems to offer you most of what you want. If you can't seem to make up your mind because your choices seem so equal, then go with your feeling that a certain school is the right one for you. It is important to feel good about the college you attend.

How Do You Complete the Admissions Process?

Once you have made your final decision, send notification to the school that you accept its offer of admission along with all the other required paperwork. Be sure to notify the other schools that you will not be accepting their offers of admission so your places can go to other students. Finally, tell your counselor and the teachers who wrote recommendations for you where you will be attending college and thank them for their assistance in helping you gain admittance to college.

Appendix A: Suggested Reference Books

College Guidebooks

College guidebooks give you a quick overview of hundreds of colleges. They have information about admissions, costs, selectivity, student life, and the college environment and present profiles of the freshman class for each college. These books are usually updated each year; use the latest edition for reliable information. You can find the following guidebooks and many others at your high school and at public libraries and bookstores.

Barron's Profiles of American Colleges. Woodbury, New York: Barron's Education Series, Inc.

The College Handbook. New York: College Board Publications.

The Complete Book of Colleges. New York: Random House/Princeton Review.

The Fiske Guide to Colleges. New York: Random House.

Kaplan Newsweek College Catalog. New York: Kaplan Books.

Lovejoy's College Guide. New York: Macmillan.

Peterson's 4 Year Colleges. Princeton, New Jersey: Peterson's.

Guidebooks on Academic Programs and Majors

Specialty guidebooks give you more information than college guidebooks do about academic programs and majors at a large number of colleges.

Index of Majors and Graduate Degrees. New York: College Board Publications.

Orchard House's 4-Year College Admissions Index of Majors and Sports. Granville, Ohio: Orchard House.

Financial Aid Books

Prospective college students should look at several books on financial aid because it is such a complex topic. To be useful, these books must have *recent* information on financial aid programs.

College Money Handbook. Princeton, New Jersey: Peterson's.

Don't Miss Out: The Ambitious Student's Guide to Financial Aid. Alexandria, Virginia: Octameron Associates.

Loans and Grants from Uncle Sam. Alexandria, Virginia: Octameron Associates.

Paying for College Without Going Broke. New York: Random House/Princeton Review.

Need a Lift? gives information about military and other scholarships that is especially helpful for students who are dependents of military personnel. Write to National Emblem Sales, *Need a Lift*, Box 1050, Indianapolis, Indiana 46206. Include three dollars for the book.

The Student Guide—Financial Aid from the U.S. Department of Education tells about federal financial aid programs and now to apply for them. For a free copy call 1-800-4-FED-AID.

Test Study Guides

These books, available at bookstores, or from test publishers, are for students who want help in preparing for college admissions tests:

Cracking the ACT. New York: Random House/Princeton Review.

Cracking the SAT and PSAT. New York: Random House/Princeton Review.

Getting into the ACT. Iowa City, Iowa: ACT.

Kaplan: SAT and PSAT. New York: Simon and Schuster.

The following publications feature actual tests:

Real SAT II: Subject Tests. New York: College Board Publications.

10 Real SATs. New York: College Board Publications.

Retired sample test booklets are available from ACT. (See the ACT Assessment Web site at http://www.act.org for information.)

Essay Writing Books

These books give strategies on how to write college application essays, and may include sample essays:

The Best College Admission Essays. New York: Arco Publishers.

How to Write a Winning College Application Essay. Rockland, California: Prima Publishing.

The College Application Essay. New York: College Board Publications.

Sports Scholarship Guides

Student athletes need to know the rules for finding sports scholarships. *NCAA Guide for the College-Bound Student* is a free booklet that has information on academic eligibility, core-course requirements, and recruitment. It is available by calling 1-800-638-3731. Here is another useful source of information:

Winning Athletic Scholarships: Guaranteeing Your Academic Eligibility for College Sports Scholarships. New York: Random House/Princeton Review.

Guides to College Life

Once you have been admitted to college, you'll want to learn what college life is like. Many of the following guides to college life are written by recent college students:

Gottesman, Greg, and Friends. *College Survival: A Crash Course for Students by Students*. New York: Macmillan.

Sponholtz, Melanie, and others. *The College Companion: Real Students' True Stories, Good Advice*. New York: Random House/Princeton Review.

Tyler, Suzette. *Been There Should've Done That! 500 Tips for Making the Most of College*. Haslett, Michigan: Front Porch Press.

Appendix B: Suggested Web Sites

Cybersurfers who are well acquainted with the Internet can find an abundance of information about college admissions on the Web.

General Information Web Sites

On your first visits to Web sites related to college admissions, you will find it helpful to explore sites that have information on a wide variety of topics including college admissions test strategies, financial aid, searching for the right college, college applications, scholarship searches, and individual colleges. The following sites are good places to start:

- ACT Assessment: http://www.act.org

- College Board: http://www.collegeboard.org

- CollegeEdge: http://www.collegeedge.com

- Kaplan: http://www.kaplan.com

- Peterson's: http://www.petersons.com

- *U.S. News*: http://www4.usnews.com

College Cost Calculators

The following Web sites, as well as general information sites, provide formulas so that you and your family can calculate your Expected Family Contribution:

- FinAid: http://www.finaid.org/calculators

- Sallie Mae: http://www.salliemae.com/calculators

Financial Aid Resources

The U.S. Department of Education offers easy-to-understand information on financial aid programs of the federal government at the Office of Postsecondary Education's homepage: http://www.ed.gov/offices/OPE/. The following booklets are available at this site:

- *The Student Guide: Financial Aid from the U.S. Department of Education*

- *Funding Your Education*

- *Looking for Student Aid*

The "Financial Aid Information Page," created by Mark Kantrowitz, has links to almost every financial aid Web site on the Internet. This is a good starting point for cyber-surfers to investigate financial aid: http://www.finaid.org.

Financial Aid Applications

You can now apply for financial aid from your home or school computers using the Free Application for Federal Student Aid (FAFSA):

- http://www.fafsa.ed.gov/ (on-line)

- http://www.ed.gov/offices/OPE/express.html (download)

College Applications

In the future, college applications may be paperless. It already is possible to use the Web when applying to college:

- CollegeBoard/College Link: http://www.collegeboard.org http://www.collegelink.com

- CollegeEdge Web Apps.: http://apply.collegeedge.com

- Common Application: http://nassp.org

- Peterson's: http://www.collegequest.com

- Princeton Review: http://www.weapply.com

College Web Sites

Most college Web sites can be accessed through http://www.(enter school name here).edu. You can also visit

Web sites, like the following, that list the homepages of colleges: http://www.utexas.edu/world/univ/state.

Admissions Tests

The Web sites of major college admissions test companies offer information about test strategies, test dates, and scoring and sample tests. It is also possible to register for these tests on-line.

- ACT: http://www.act.org

- SAT I and SAT II: http://www.collegeboard.org

College Sports

The NCCA guide for student athletes and other information about playing sports in college are available at http:www.ncaa.org/cbsa.

Appendix C: Glossary

ACT Assessment is one of the two major college admissions tests. The ACT has four tests: English, mathematics, reading, and science reasoning.

Advanced Placement (AP) Tests are tests that high school students take in order to gain college credit or placement in advanced courses at college.

Class rank is the rating that compares a student's grade point average to those of other students in the class. It is often a factor in college admissions.

Cooperative Education Programs let students combine their college studies with off-campus jobs.

Early action is an admissions option that lets students find out early if they have been accepted to a college but that does not require a commitment to attend the school until the regular admissions acceptance deadline.

Early decision is an admissions option that gives early notification of acceptance and requires students to make a commitment to attend the admitting college.

Expected Family Contribution is the amount of money students applying for financial aid and their families are expected to pay toward the cost of attending college.

Federal Supplemental Educational Opportunity Grants (FSEOGs) are grants administered by colleges to help students with the greatest financial need.

Free Application for Federal Student Aid (FAFSA) is the form used to apply for financial aid from federal and state governments and colleges.

Ivy league schools are Brown, Columbia, Cornell, Dartmouth, Harvard, the University of Pennsylvania, Princeton, and Yale. These selective schools were once members of their own sports league.

National Merit Scholarship is a scholarship that is awarded to students on the basis of their scores on the PSAT/NMSQT and other factors.

Pell Grant is the largest federal grant program for undergraduates. It is a need-based grant that is awarded to all students who qualify.

Perkins Loans are low-interest federal loans that are awarded to students with financial need. They are administered by colleges. No interest is paid on these loans while students are in college.

PLAN is a test that uses the same format as the ACT. It is normally taken by students in their sophomore year as a counseling tool.

PLUS Loans are loans made by the government and a variety of lending agencies to credit-approved parents to help them pay for their children's college education.

Preliminary Scholastic Aptitude Test/National Merit Scholarship Qualifying Test (PSAT/NMSQT) is a multiple choice test composed of verbal and math sections like the SAT I. Besides letting students see what the SAT I is like, it is the qualifying test for the National Merit Scholarship program.

Rolling admissions is an admissions plan in which decisions about accepting or rejecting applicants are made by colleges shortly after receiving applications.

SAT I is a college admissions test that has verbal and math sections and is required for admission to many colleges.

SAT II: Subject Tests are college admissions tests of students' knowledge or skills in different subjects and of their ability to apply that knowledge.

Stafford Student Loans are guaranteed federal loans that allow students to borrow money from the federal government or other lending agencies.

Student Aid Report (SAR) is sent to applicants who have applied for financial aid. It tells them what their Expected Family Contributions are.

Viewbook is a book or brochure with pictures that a college distributes to give prospective students information about the college.

Waiting list is a list of students who are neither accepted nor rejected by a college but who will be accepted if students who were admitted decide not to attend the college.

Work-study program is a program in which college students work part-time at jobs while attending school. The program is funded by the federal government, state governments, and colleges.